CW00501382

First published in Gr
by The Sim

Authors: Asim Khan & Toyris Miah
Cover design & illustrations by: Anisa Mohammed

Book design by The Simple Seerah Ltd.

Published by The Simple Seerah Ltd.

Printed by Mega Print

Printed in Turkiye

ISBN 978-1-7399095-1-2

www.simpleseerah.com | info@simpleseerah.com

The Simple Seerah Ltd, 124 City Road, London, EC1V 2NX

Stealing Is Forbidden

In Islam, stealing is considered to be a terrible crime and there are clear commandments which tell us not to do so. It is even considered a sin to buy products if you know they are stolen. With this in mind, we kindly ask you to ensure that you do not copy, scan, photograph or record the contents of this book in any shape or form and then share it with others.

If you receive a PDF of this book, please do not share it with others, as the PDF is stolen property.

You are more than welcome to lend or gift your own physical copy of this book to anyone of your choosing.

To purchase a genuine copy of this book please visit www.simpleseerah.com

If you are unable to purchase your own copy, please contact us via our website and we will send you a copy (terms and conditions apply). Please see our website for further details.

The Simple Seerah – Part One Supporters

Asif Hayat,
Abid Ansari,
Keeran Sachania,
Shahaid Rashid,
Mr Mohammad Ashraf,
Mrs Sameena Ashraf,
Maryum Alnur Anisur Rehman,
Afshan Khan,
Mujtaba Khan,
Saira Afsar,
Mohammad Hussain,
Edu-Vision Wales
Aslam shafeek,
S Shuab Ahmed,
Abdul Sabur Tafadar,
Abubaker Khan,
Seedat Family,
Rahila Ibrahim,
Asma Zafrani,
Mohammed Zakaria Miah,
Khurshid Iqbal,
Arshed Iqbal,
Mohammed Joytun,
Rabeya Khatun

I have to start by thanking my awesome friend and sidekick, Toyris Miah. From pitching the idea of a novel-like Seerah for young adults, to helping me edit the work, and all the logistical grind that goes behind self-publishing, he was as important to this book getting done as I was. Jazakallahukhayr my brother!

Special thanks to my parents, and then my wife, Sobia Khan, for supporting me in this project and keeping the munchkins out of my hair so I could spend time in the library. Jazakallahukhayr my dear.

Finally, thanks to Malika Kahn for being a great writing coach to me, our incredible illustrator Anisa, Zaheer Khatri (from Learning Roots) for your detailed feedback, and Siraj for proofreading the manuscript.

May Allah reward you all and bless you with a spot in Paradise next to the Prophet Muhammad ﷺ.

Asim Khan

Contents

Author's Note

All praise is due to Allah Almighty, and may peace and salutations be upon His final Messenger, Muhammad ﷺ.

I remember completing a book on the life of the Prophet ﷺ for the very first time. As I read the last few pages I remember being moved to tears and thinking, *why on earth am I only reading this now? I'm in university, studying pharmacy, why haven't I studied the life of this amazing man already?* I felt like I never really knew who the Prophet was until I completed that book. I felt regret. *Why had it taken this long for me to learn something so important?*

Looking back, I realise that it wasn't *all* my fault. It was about access too. There weren't many (if any) Seerah books written in English for young adults. The ones that were available were very detailed, academic, and…well, not very interesting to read! This is why I was instantly drawn to the idea of writing a novel-like Seerah book for young adults. I want every Muslim, young or really young, to know who the Prophet ﷺ was, appreciate his message and struggle, and have a burning desire to follow his example.

I pray that Allah allows this work to achieve such a noble goal.

Asim Khan

Also by Asim Khan

The Simple Seerah - Part One

The Heart of the Qur'an
Tafsir of Surah Yasin

The Kingdom of God
Tafsir of Surah al-Mulk

Available on Amazon and at all good book stores.

Shaykh Dr Omar Suleiman Foreword

All praise is due to Allah Almighty, and may peace and salutations be upon His final Messenger, Muhammad ﷺ.

Had you lived in the time of the Prophet ﷺ, you would have longed to see him each and every day. You would have immensely enjoyed his smiles, speeches, and recreational activities with children, regardless of whether these children were his or yours.

The truth is, the closest we can get to the Prophet ﷺ is to read about his life. By studying it, not only does our love for him increase, but we also long to be among his Companions in the next world.

One of the main objectives of The Simple Seerah is to make it easy for the young generation of Muslims today to understand and learn from the life of the Prophet ﷺ. The novel-like language and storytelling structure used throughout the book is easy and engaging for most youngsters and even adults. Combined with the brilliant illustrations, you're transported to ancient Arabia to witness the trials and challenges of the early Muslims.

I believe that this book will help you transition from *only* knowing about Muhammad ﷺ to knowing him and loving him and feel what it was like to be a companion of his in this life and strive to be companions of his in the next.

To ensure that every event mentioned in this book is genuine, Ustadh Asim Khan has only mentioned events about the Prophet that can be backed up by the classical books of Seerah like Ibn Ishaq, Ibn Hisham, and Ibn Kathir. This is incredibly reassuring for all of us as it ensures what we are reading is accurate and not fiction.

I ask Allah Almighty to accept this work and place Barakah in it. May He bless the authors and their families, students, and friends who supported them throughout the journey of producing "The Simple Seerah".

Shaykh Dr Omar Suleiman
Sep 2022 | 1444AH

Our Principles

Everyone loves a good story, it's just that we don't call them stories anymore, we call them movies and dramas. In a world of wizards, *Hobbits*, *Jedis* and *Marvel* superheroes, you could easily be led to believe that the best stories are those written (or filmed) in our times, right? But what if I were to tell you that in your hands right now lies the greatest story ever to be told? A story like no other— a story that is an inspiration to all of humanity?

This is a story of how an orphan child who lived in the deserts of Arabia fourteen-hundred years ago became the most powerful and beloved human being to ever walk the face of this earth— a story of a true superhero. This is the story of none other than the Prophet Muhammad ﷺ, which is known as *Seerah* in Arabic.

Although many books have been written about his blessed life, this book is the first of its kind. It lifts the raw narrative as told in classical *Seerah* literature, which spans over a thousand years, and translates it into a flowing, descriptive and enchanting narrative that is engaging for both young and old.

Here are some of the key principles we followed in producing this ground-breaking work:

1. Every quote of the Prophet ﷺ and Companions found in this book is a direct historical narration taken from the classical works of *Seerah*.[1]

---

[1] See Endnotes for the complete list

2. Readers are strongly encouraged to say *sallallahu alayhi wassalam* whenever the Prophet is mentioned. It's at the top of every page to help remind you.

3. No event or incident about the Prophet ﷺ falls into the realm of fiction. There are, however, added details that are extrapolations based on the raw *Seerah* narrative, verses from the Qur'an, and other Prophetic narrations (Hadith) as found in the classical sources. These details are there to help transport the reader to the time of the Prophet ﷺ by adding ambience and environment to each scene.

4. This book is not meant to be a comprehensive narrative of the *Seerah*. The details we believe are the most inspirational to the younger audience have been given priority due to the nature of this book.

5. This work is based on the most authoritative classical sources in the *Seerah* literature. A full list can be found in the Bibliography and Endnotes.

Lastly, the Prophet ﷺ presented Islam to the people of the time using the language of the time. Here we are trying to relay the message of the *Seerah* to the people of today using the language of today while retaining the everlasting message and values of the beloved of Allah.

May the eternal peace and blessings of Allah be upon him.

Asim Khan
Toyris Miah

THE SIMPLE
SEERAH

PART TWO

Asim Khan & Toyris Miah
Illustrated By: Anisa Mohammed

Chapter 1
The Warm Embrace of Madinah

Ten days had passed since Prophet Muhammad ﷺ and Abu Bakr had left Makkah with bounty hunters hot on their heels. So far, only one had managed to track them down— Suraaqa; but after seeing the miraculous way in which the pair were being protected, he let them go in peace. Eventually, the Prophet and his best friend came across a modest Bedouin dwelling. The scattered tents, fixed in the bronze sand, were a welcome sight in the sun-scorched landscape. They rested here for some time before setting off again to complete the migration.

"Where have you been? You just missed them!" Umm Ma'bad's voice startled her husband as he ducked underneath the flap to enter their tent.

"Never mind where I've been," he said, giving her a long stare while fanning himself with the tail of his dusty turban. "Where in the world did *this* come from?" He pointed at a half-empty clay bowl resting neatly on a worn-out cloth. Inside the bowl was the source of his confusion: creamy white milk glistening with freshness. *But how?* Their flock had hardly anywhere left to graze, and the goat that remained behind was far too skinny to produce milk.

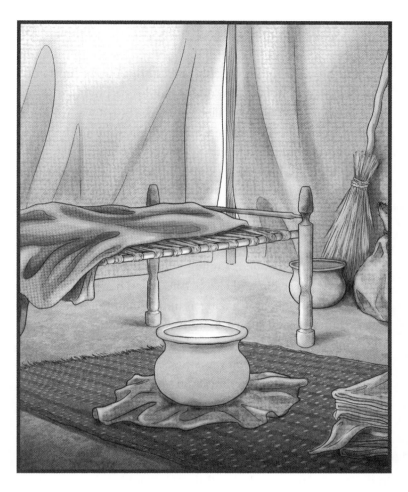

"A blessed man was here today." Umm Ma'bad explained. "He caused milk to flow from our goat— who you know as well as I do is well beyond any milking!" She walked over to her husband, pulling his wrists into her hands. Though her face had all the signs of old age, her mind had refused to grow old, as did her wit and strength. Not much could slip past this Bedouin woman; except on this occasion, she had failed to connect the dots.

"Oh, he was truly blessed," she said, staring into her husband's eyes. "He had a radiant face and a handsome physique. Thick eyelashes bordered his large black eyes. His beard was thick too, and his brows fine and arched." Her words spun in the air, as eloquent as any Makkan poet.

Her husband listened carefully, intrigued by the meticulous attention she had paid to this stranger's every feature. He squinted as he wracked his brain, trying to think of who this person could possibly have been.

"An air of dignity surrounded him when he was silent," Umm Ma'bad continued, smiling in wonderment, "and when he spoke, he was calm and clear." She raised her head skywards with a faraway look, as if gazing at him in that moment. "When you see him from a distance, he is the most handsome of people, and when you are face to face with him, you discover that he is also the kindest. His speech was sweet—"

"Wait a minute…" Her husband's hands flew over his mouth as he suddenly realized who the mysterious man was. Before he could say another word, his wife ploughed on.

"He had a companion with him too, and every time he would speak, that friend would listen silently to what he said, and when he requested something, he would rush to carry out the order."

"That was the man from the Quraysh I've been hearing about from passersby!" he burst out, his hand now clutching his turban, revealing his bald head.

"You mean…" Umm Ma'bad gasped. "*The one they're calling a Prophet?!*"

Silence filled the room as they contemplated what this encounter meant for them. *Are we now in danger too? What should someone who is visited by a Prophet of God do?* These questions and more swirled around in their minds until, finally, her husband broke the silence. He straightened his worn-out robe, adjusting his turban upright as he walked over to the bowl of milk.

"If I ever have the opportunity, I will certainly join his religion," he vowed. Umm Ma'bad nodded back to him with a hearty smile. They hoped that wherever the Prophet was headed, he would receive the welcome he deserved.[1]

§

Abu Lahab had been enjoying a mouth-watering feast in the company of his loud friends when his no-good servant reminded him of the meeting he had to attend. "Is it time *already?*" he spat through a mouthful of food. The last thing he wanted to do was think about his troublemaker of a nephew and his band of rebels— at least that's what they were in his eyes. Abu Lahab wiped his greasy mouth, gathered his robe, and stomped to Darun Nadwah.

Darun Nadwah was the grand meeting place of the leaders of Quraysh— the mighty hall in which they hatched their petty schemes. Their meetings tended to be a civilized affair, though on this particularly warm evening, the thick stone walls of the assembly house shook with the furious voices of those inside. Everyone was upset.

"And now, those pesky Muslims have found yet another safe haven," Abu Jahl said, summarising the series of disappointments they had faced. "I swear by the goddess Laat! If things continue this way— Utbah, Abu Sufyan, listen up, you two."

Abu Sufyan cleared his throat. "We're here and listening," he replied. "No need to get angry with *us.*"

"If things continue this way, we're destined for humiliation!" For the first time, Abu Jahl sounded afraid, not just angry. It was as though he could see where things were heading.

The tribe leaders were still bitter that they were unable to thwart Muhammad's departure from Makkah. Their assassination attempt was as much of a failure as their search parties; the only thing they returned with was news that Muhammad was bound for the city of Yathrib.

"Those bounty hunters were a useless bunch!" Abu Lahab said, his face burning with rage. "I heard that Suraaqa— so-called *Assassin of Arabia* —actually caught the pair of them, but then let them go!"

Abu Jahl stared at him. "*What?* What do you mean?"

"I mean," snapped Abu Lahab, "he's now one of them."

Abu Jahl's eyes almost bolted out of their sockets.

"This is worse than when they fled to Abyssinia," Utbah sighed, massaging his wrinkled forehead.

"I mean, Yathrib is in our own backyard," Abu Jahl sneered. "*If* they establish themselves there, the consequences could be dire."

The men nodded grimly, some groaning in frustration. Their worries were certainly not unfounded. If the Muslims were allowed to thrive in Yathrib, they would have the opportunity to take control of the northern trade routes, cutting off the Quraysh from one of their economic lifelines.

Abu Sufyan narrowed his eyes in thought. "We depend on those northern routes, and Muhammad knows this…"

"Are you saying choosing to go to Yathrib was strategic?" mused Abu Lahab, as he beckoned a servant over for more wine. "I suppose he is a businessman, and—"

"Who cares what their motives were," Abu Jahl interrupted. "They have their leader with them now! Who knows what the lot of them are planning…"

"Revenge, probably," said Abu Sufyan.

"Well, we can't just sit here and wait to see what happens!" cried Utbah.

"Precisely!" Abu Jahl slammed the table with both hands. "We have to do something about them and FAST," he said, emphasizing his every word.

Agreement shone in every pair of eyes that met his hardened gaze. It wasn't enough that Muhammad and his people had been forced to flee the city, leaving behind their relatives, livelihoods, and homes. The Quraysh were blinded by hate, and nothing short of complete removal of the Prophet and everything he stood for would satisfy them.

§

It had been twelve gruelling days since the Prophet and Abu Bakr had left Makkah. Trying to stay ahead of the assassins who craved the hefty bounty on their heads was taking its toll. It hurt the Prophet that the people who pursued him were the same people he had known his entire life—people who once loved and respected him; people he hoped would have been eager to embrace his message.

Now only a day or so away from Yathrib, the Prophet looked ahead to where the blue sky met the golden sea of sand, stretching on and on, beckoning to a new beginning. Although he had left his beloved hometown with no luggage, he carried with him hope that weighed heavy. Allah had granted them a way out of a harmful situation, and though he was unsure how the people of Yathrib would react upon his arrival, he trusted in Allah's plan.

§

In Yathrib, the Muslims were growing restless. The Prophet's arrival was well overdue. Each morning after the dawn prayer (*Fajr*), the new converts, accompanied by the migrants of Makkah, eagerly went out to look for him. They congregated on the city's outskirts, praising Allah as they stood waiting in the cool shadows of date palms, each one hoping to be the first to lay eyes on the man they had heard so much about.

They waited until the sun reached its midpoint in the sky, stealing the shade and scorching the sand. This is when their camels, half-hidden by loads of freshly picked dates, stood up and shifted uncomfortably, signalling it was time for them to head back home. As they set off back home reluctantly, the learned among them recited verses of the Qur'an to reassure them all.

> *"O believers! Seek comfort in patience and prayer. Allah is truly with those who are patient."*
> **[Qur'an 2:153]**

A group of Jewish men nearby had been peering into the horizon from their small fortress. They too were interested in seeing this Prophet of God, though they were not convinced. They thought to themselves: *how could the Almighty send a prophet of Arab descent and not from the children of the Israelites?* Nonetheless, from this height, the gentle breeze allowed them to stay out a little longer than those on the ground.

The first to notice a glimmer in the desert was Solomon. He squinted, leaning forward to get a better look.

"Ezra! Look. Over there."

"You're seeing things, aren't you?" Ezra chuckled. "Old age catching up with you, eh?"

"You fool! Use the blessings God has given you and look over there!" The man pointed insistently to a faraway point on the horizon.

Ezra leaned over the balcony of the fort and caught a glimpse of what appeared to be white-robed travellers in the distance. "Well, well, well. For once, you may be right!"

Solomon waved off his teasing remarks and ran as quickly as he could to the other side of the roof overlooking the city. He wanted to be the first to make the announcement.

"Aws and Khazraj, your king has finally arrived!" he yelled.

Those in earshot turned around in excitement. Raising their hands to block out the intense rays of the sun, they looked in the direction the elderly Jewish man was pointing. The white garments of the Prophet and Abu Bakr now stood out as bright specks flanked by the dark mountains and quiet desert in the distance.

"He's not a *king*!" one of the new converts shouted back. "That there is the Messenger of Allah!" he said with an indulgent smile.

Monday | September 622 CE

The Muslims dispersed, eager to share the exciting news. One man burst into his home, panting to catch his breath before yelling, "He has arrived! Hurry, otherwise we'll miss it!"

"Who's arrived?" asked his wife. "Oh! You mean— *Subhan Allah!*"

His family jumped up, racing to and fro to gather their shawls, drums, and any refreshments at hand. In the rush, the oldest child wrestled on the robe of the youngest. "Wait, let's swap!" he cried, chasing after his little brother, who stumbled along with the garment trailing on the ground.

§

Prophet Muhammad and Abu Bakr were met with a surprising sight as they neared the city on top of their camels. The Muslims had mobilised themselves to give an unforgettable reception. A group of men from the Aws and Khazraj Tribes lined the entrance, fully dressed in armour with swords raised to the sky in salute. They wanted to show the Prophet that their oath at Aqabah was not empty; they were ready to protect him.

The armed men began to form a procession with some of their mounts. Friendly faces weaved in between the marching soldiers to greet them. Those who had not yet seen the Prophet rushed to Abu Bakr first, thinking *he* was the Prophet— an easy mistake considering Prophet Muhammad's humble nature. Noticing this, Abu Bakr unwrapped his shawl and held it over the Prophet's head to cast some shade over him.

"*Assalamualaykum O Messenger of Allah!*" cried a bare-legged elderly man, his turban half-unwound. The Prophet smiled in his face. The people then realized who the Prophet was and were amazed by his modesty. They quickly rushed over to greet him.

Children raced forward with joyful grins while the youth hung from the trees, waving banners and palm leaves in welcome. Some stood on rooftops while others emerged from around every corner, joining the crowd and filling the area with a buzz of excitement. Several familiar faces looked at the Prophet, their eyes moistened with tears when their gazes met his. They were his followers from Makkah who had already migrated. The sight was as overwhelming for the Prophet just as it was uplifting. As the crowd slowly ventured back into the city, he recalled some of the Revelation he had received in Makkah that foretold this migration:

"O My servants who believe! Be mindful of your Lord. Those who do good in this world will have a good reward. And Allah's earth is spacious. Only those who endure patiently will be given their reward without limit."

[Qur'an 39:10]

The measured throb of a drum resounded, each beat building into a simple rhythm. Women and children began singing their welcome in a song that would carry on many centuries later in memory of that happy day when, like the full moon, Prophet Muhammad appeared before his people.

O the full moon rose over us
From the valley of Wadaa
And we must show gratefulness
When called to Allah

O Messenger sent to us
With commands to be obeyed
You have brought this city nobleness
Welcome, O noble caller to Allah's way

News of his arrival spread throughout the entire city. Many ran out to greet him as he rode in, begging him to accept their hospitality. "Stay with us, O Messenger of Allah!" they said, reaching out to pull his camel's halter.

"Let the camel go her way," was the Prophet's gentle reply as the animal, which he had nicknamed Qaswa, strolled past the crowd. "She is being guided by Allah," he explained.

Qaswa wandered gracefully into a stony courtyard near the middle of the oasis. It had once been a burial ground, now used for drying dates. The camel walked to a spot and knelt, her front legs buckling, followed by her hind legs until finally, she sank to the ground with a soft grunt as if to say, "This far and no further."

The migration (*hijrah*) was officially complete. Prophet Muhammad dismounted and looked around the area. "Who owns this land?" he asked.

"It belongs to two orphans," someone replied. The man, who was their guardian, explained that the two young boys were from the same Khazraj Tribe to which the Prophet's great-grandmother had belonged. The similarities between their backgrounds and his childhood made the selected spot seem significant in more ways than one.

"Please, take this land as a gift," the children's guardian insisted. But the Prophet told him he would rather pay for it in full. With a smile, the Prophet announced that his mosque,

Masjid al-Nabawi, would be built on this very spot. This unlikely patch of land would become the centre of the believers' world.

The joy of walking among his followers freely and openly was enough to make the Prophet forget about the threat of the Quraysh—at least for the time being. Many rushed to offer their homes to him. A very distant relative of the Prophet, called Abu Ayyub, acted quickly and lifted the saddle off Qaswa, carrying it into his home nearby. "A man must follow his saddle," the Prophet said light-heartedly. And so Abu Ayyub became Prophet Muhammad's first host.

Another convert named Asad took hold of the halter, leading Qaswa somewhere to rest. The people were eager to make the Prophet feel right at home.

But not everyone in Yathrib was happy. Abdullah ibn Ubay was a veteran tribal leader with long-standing ambitions of becoming the king of Yathrib. Though he belonged to the Khazraj Tribe, he played the role of peacemaker between them and the Aws— a role that helped him string the beads of his own crown. Or so he thought. From the shadows of his front room, he adjusted the curtain to catch a better look at the cheering crowds encircling the traveller from Makkah. He took one long hard look at Muhammad's face and muttered under his breath, "Prophet or not, no man will stand in my way…" He then looked at the people, their eyes glittering in admiration.

"May they all go blind!" he said, his top lip curling in disgust.

Allah the Almighty has promised in the Qur'an that "with hardship comes ease". The Prophet and his Companions had to endure thirteen years of hardship and suffering. The decision to migrate was a difficult and dangerous one, but it demonstrated their unwavering trust in Allah. Their longstanding sacrifices were not overlooked by Allah, and when the time was right, He opened up for them the doors to peace, safety, and belonging. As for the thirteen years of struggle, it had made them a source of inspiration for the future followers of Prophet Muhammad.

Chapter 2
Laying The Foundations

Half a century had passed since the Year of the Elephant. The Prophet had now reached the age of fifty-three. Grey streaks flecked his long beard. Still, he was remarkably fit and energetic, wasting no time to get to work establishing the new society. He hardly seemed to need sleep, spending his nights in prayer and his days working side by side with his followers to build the mosque. The Prophet kept his hair braided into four plaits to keep tidy during this demanding time. Each day, they cleared stones and shrubs from the courtyard, replanting the trees elsewhere. For the structure, they shaped bricks from mud and wove palm leaves to create a roof. Two small homes were also to be constructed at the mosque's eastern wall for the Prophet's wives, Sawdah and the newlywed Aisha.

The whole building took seven months to complete. Constructing a public symbol of their faith after thirteen years of struggle felt like a victory for the Muslims from Makkah. It was a meaningful milestone for the Muslim community as a whole.

"*Subhan Allah!*" The Muslims exclaimed on the day they entered the newly completed mosque. They weaved between the columns holding up the roofed section, footsteps pattering over the beaten clay floor. Looking around, they admired the modest structure. "At last, a peaceful place to gather." Together, they admired the modest structure. "At last, a peaceful place to gather," the migrants smiled at each other. Lining up in the open courtyard, the Muslims faced north towards Jerusalem for the first prayer in their official place of worship.

In the same way that each brick had been stacked together to form a solid wall, Prophet Muhammad wished the same for his followers—after all, strength lay in unity. They were now recognized as two distinct groups: the Emigrants (Muhajirun) from Makkah and the Supporters (Ansar), the converts from

Yathrib. The Prophet set up a ground-breaking policy that made every member of the two groups into brothers and sisters. Each Muhajir was bound by a pact to an Ansar, who was to help them settle down in the best way possible.

During his sermons in the mosque, the Prophet advised them, "Remember that a Muslim is a brother to a Muslim. He should neither deceive nor lie to him nor forsake him in his time of need. Everything belonging to a Muslim is protected by Allah's law: his honour, blood, and property."[2] The Ansar embraced this policy wholeheartedly, going above and beyond to share their homes and livelihood with the Muhajirun.

One day, they approached the Prophet with a proposal. "O Messenger of Allah, distribute the palm groves between the Muhajirun and us."

They thought this was a brilliant idea and were surprised when the Prophet disapproved. He did not want the Muhajirun to live on handouts or feel like they were a burden on others. After a brief pause, they suggested something else. "Then how about we allow them to work on the farms and split the harvests with them?" Much to their delight, the Prophet agreed to this.

The Muhajirun were grateful for the opportunity. Each day, they set off early to earn their keep at the farms. They soon noticed something strange— the Ansar were racing to finish most of the work before they could!

"O Messenger of Allah, we have never seen people like this!" they said in astonishment. "They support us even though many of them are poor, and the rich among them are generous with their wealth. They work so hard on their farms yet split the harvest equally with us— they will surely take all the rewards on the Day of Judgement!"

This brought a smile to the Prophet's face. He shook his head slightly. "You will also be rewarded as long as you show them gratitude and pray for them,"[3] he assured the group of men.

The Ansar broke out into smiles of their own when a verse from the Heavens came down celebrating their sacrifices.

> *Those who were already established in their homes in Madinah, and rooted in faith, show love to those who migrated to them and hold no desire in their hearts for what has been given to them. They give them preference over themselves, even if they too are poor. And whoever is saved from selfishness, it is they who are truly successful.*
> **[Qur'an 59:9]**

Despite the incredible hospitality, settling in was not easy for the Muslims from Makkah.

One morning, the Prophet asked Aisha to check up on her father, Abu Bakr, and some of the other Companions. With fruits in hand, she trudged along the dusty roads, keeping to the shade of the mud-bricked homes. Faint noises filled the surroundings as the people of Yathrib began their day's work. The young woman soon caught the attention of a group of ladies. She was noticeably taller than other women, but that wasn't why they had stopped in their tracks. It was because of her newfound status as the wife of the Prophet; the story behind it often left people in awe.

"Peace be upon you, Lady Aisha," the ladies greeted as they crossed paths.

"And on you be peace, my sisters," Aisha replied.

"Sisters?!" remarked the eldest of the women. "Rather, being the wife of the Messenger of Allah makes you a mother to all Believers." She smiled warmly. "God has truly blessed you."

Aisha returned the smile and, with a polite nod, continued on her way towards a spacious front garden shaded by date palms. She could still hear them talking in the distance. "She's the one Allah showed the Prophet as a bride in a dream, you know…"

Aisha lowered her head out of shyness and tried not to listen any further. She stepped into the entrance of a few cosily packed houses. A ray of sunshine filtered in through the leaves above, brightening her mood as she followed it into the courtyard. There she found Abu Bakr lying on a straw mat, one hand over his forehead. Two other men were half-asleep in the corner.

"Peace be upon you!" she greeted while approaching. "How are you doing, my father?"

"My child…" he answered faintly, his body barely moving.

"What is it?" she leaned over studying his face with concern.

"Words fail to capture my pain."

"Are you unwell?"

Turning his face away from his daughter's worried look, Abu Bakr uttered lines of poetry under his breath.

"Each morning, each man's children greet him good day,
But today death is nearer than his sandal's strap."

"Oh father, please don't say that," she said, lightly stroking his head.

Aisha looked at the others in the room, realizing that they also appeared extremely weak. One man rolled over onto his back. It was Bilal, the former slave who was freed by Abu Bakr what seemed like many years ago. She asked him how he felt, but his only response was to gaze above with his feverish eyes as he expressed his pain through poetry.

"O shall I ever sleep the night again
Amid the shrubs and grass that outside Makkah grow,
I long to drink the waters from the well of Majannah,
And to be surrounded by those glorious mountains again..."

Many who migrated from Makkah were either struck by homesickness or physical illness due to the change of climate. In Bilal's case, he seemed to be afflicted with both at once. His usually strong voice quivered as he conveyed the heaviness of his heart. Though his body was weak, his faith was as firm as ever, but like most, he longed for the familiarity of home.

Aisha's mind raced to find the right words to console them. She held her father's hand. "I know no place is like Makkah, but this rich and fertile city is our new home. We just need some time to get used to the climate..."

She opened her water pouch, gently lifting her father's head to pour a few sips between his chapped lips. "May Allah cure you and bring relief," she said, making sure he was comfortable before heading back.

Aisha returned home in a very different mood than when she had left that morning. The Prophet was quick to notice the concern etched on her face. "I have bad news to share," she said. Despite not fully understanding the poetry the men had uttered in their feverish states, she related it word-for-word, effectively conveying their sense of displacement.

She was pleasantly surprised that the Prophet appreciated Abu Bakr and Bilal's frankness. He nodded, contemplating the situation. He understood the Muhajirun's predicament, knowing that although they were glad to be free from the oppressive Quraysh, their freedom had come at the cost of giving up their homes and livelihoods. Most of them had been in the business of trading, while Yathrib's main work was date farming. They were certainly out of their element, more so when the shifting humidity brought with it illnesses their bodies were unaccustomed to.

"Perhaps the Messenger of Allah can pray for the Muhajirun," Aisha suggested, looking at him earnestly. "Allah always listens to your prayers."

The Prophet gave her an endearing smile, then raised his hands towards the sky and prayed, "O Allah! Make Madinah beloved to us just like Makkah is, or even more so. Grant us good health and place blessings in the fruit and grain of this city."[4]

By renaming Yathrib, the city officially shed its old identity as a troubled land for a new title that fostered the hope of a bright future: *Madinatun Nabi*, the Prophet's City—Madinah for short.

Allah granted the Prophet's prayer, and his Companions' health soon improved. As they worked together and bonded with their generous hosts, the city became so dear to them that in the years that followed, the Muslims of Makkah would never dream of leaving it.

§

As for the Prophet, he realized that the situation in Madinah was far from simple. Home to a diverse community of Muslims, pagan Arabs, and Jewish tribes, the city wasn't free from the inevitable clashes and tribal politics. He also had to deal with the jealousy, greed, and desire for power now directed at him— attitudes he had not really experienced in Makkah. He did, however, have faint childhood memories of his grandfather, Abdul Muttalib, dealing with similar matters in front of the Ka'bah. Little did he know back then that one day, he would be in much the same position— not as a tribal leader, but as a leader for humanity.

Although the old rivalry between the tribes of Aws and Khazraj had simmered down ever since their newfound faith, sometimes the tribal grudge would resurface from something as trivial as misinterpreting someone's tone of voice. One of the Companions had been walking to the mosque when he heard two men bickering nearby.

"Where is your respect?"

"Who are you to demand respect?" the man sneered, looking the other up and down. "Typical Aws behaviour…"

"What did you say!?" The offended man was ready to lunge when the call to prayer filled the air.

"*Allahu Akbar, Allahu Abkar,*" Bilal's voice boomed over their heads and into their hearts, cooling their tempers.

Unclenching his fist, the Khazraj tribesman stepped back and instead spat at the other man's feet before briskly walking off in a huff.

When the Prophet heard about such incidents, he realized that old habits could not be banished so easily. A lot of work still needed to be done to refine the character of his followers and strengthen their brotherhood. He did not want the kind of volatile conflicts that broke out in Makkah to be a problem here, nor did he approve of the communities disrespecting each other. It was time to establish some rules for the sake of a healthy, united society.

One late afternoon, as the air grew cool, Prophet Muhammad called for a meeting at a place known as the Garden of Banu

Saida. This leafy garden was a well-known meeting place with two wells of sweet-tasting water that people would stop and drink from when passing by. The beautiful greenery and soft breeze could calm the senses of anyone who stepped within the area. It was the perfect spot to establish the pact, an official agreement that would lay the foundation of a stable society.

The Prophet, dressed in a simple robe and turban, stood at the head of the assembly. All eyes were on him. The Muslims formed the largest crowd made up of his followers from Makkah, who had sacrificed so much, and the converts of Madinah, who had welcomed them with open arms. The leaders of the various tribes stood slightly ahead of their groups, decorating the garden with garments of bright hues and earthy tans.

"What do you think this is all about?" they asked Abu Bakr and Umar, the Prophet's two most senior Companions.

"Allah and His Messenger know best," they replied, almost in unison.

Then there were the Jewish tribes who had also migrated to Madinah many years earlier, anticipating the arrival of a new prophet as promised in their scripture. "Let's wait and see," said one of the Jewish leaders to his comrades who had asked a similar question. He stood with his arms crossed, carefully watching as the Prophet welcomed everyone.

The crowd's intrigue grew when the Prophet explained the purpose of the meeting: to present a vision for the city that he hoped they all would agree on.

"This is a pact between Muhammad—the Messenger of Allah—and the Believers of Makkah and Madinah, as well as the non-Muslims who live alongside them. We are now one united community, distinct from others, and will live together side by side."

The opening statement drew some smiles.

A man from the Ansar leaned over to whisper to his comrades, "*Alhamdulillah*! We made the right choice at Aqabah those many moons ago." They smiled warmly in agreement. The Aws and Khazraj, along with the Muharijun, were now brothers under one blue sky with a shared vision they could all work towards. A sense of optimism hung in the air. A leader as sincere as Prophet Muhammad, who valued togetherness and respect, could only invite goodness into their lives. They believed this wholeheartedly and eagerly listened to his words.

"The Believers are each other's allies. The God-fearing must stand up against whoever acts wrongfully or unjustly, or promotes sin or evil within our community. They are to unite against such people, even if it turns out to be their own children."

Earnest nods accompanied the murmurs of agreement. It became increasingly clear to the new converts that they had to learn to place the bonds of faith above the bonds of the tribe. They were now part of a cause far bigger than any of them or their tribes. However, Abdullah Ibn Ubay exchanged a bitter glance with a couple of his men. The power that Muhammad commanded, despite being a newcomer, made his blood boil. As the speech continued, he adjusted the hood of his cloak, trying to hide his frown.

"The Jews and idol-worshippers who live peacefully alongside us will receive aid and support. They will not be wronged, nor will their enemies be aided against them. You have your religion, and the Muslims have theirs."

This point impressed the Jewish leaders, who were glad that this man intended to uphold peace in this previously troubled land. However, they were not quite accepting of what the Prophet said next.

"If, however, you fall into dispute, it will be settled by Allah and His Messenger."

"Does he consider himself *our* leader, too?" a Jewish man protested. The Jewish tribes appeared civil in their interactions with the Muslims but did not accept Muhammad as a Prophet of God, mainly because he was of Arab descent. Although his characteristics and features matched the description in their scripture, they were convinced that the one they awaited would be from their own people. Noticing that every other group seemed happy with what they were hearing—especially the Muslims, all wide-eyed in admiration—the man swallowed his contempt.

The Prophet continued, "Whoever does wrong or commits treachery brings only evil on himself and his household. Those in agreement will aid each other against whoever is at war with the people of this pact. Between them are goodwill and sincerity. Ultimately, righteousness is far easier than sin."[5]

During the speech, many had unknowingly held their breath. The Prophet's eloquence captivated them, and when he finished, there was a collective pause before voices erupted in agreement. Most were pleased with his intention to unite the communities in the city, forming a stronghold that shielded Madinah from any outside dangers. The Muhajirun were especially proud to call him their leader. Their eyes glistened with emotion as they recalled the persecution they had endured in Makkah to now have finally reached this point. Prophet Muhammad was their saviour, and they were committed to doing their part to strengthen their new community.

The Jewish leaders appeared to welcome the pact. One by one, the tribe leaders echoed their consent. It proved hard to disagree with a vision that valued peace and justice. Even the likes of Abdullah Ibn Ubay pushed his way to the front of the

THE SIMPLE SEERAH - PART TWO

crowd to embrace the Prophet and loudly declare his allegiance. Seeing this shocked those who knew him. But behind the big smile strapped on his face lay a dark, twisted secret.

§

Needless to say, the ever-frustrated Quraysh did not welcome this news.

"Wasn't that place on the verge of civil war not too long ago?" Abu Jahl groaned.

"How did he manage to unite those two tribes?" Abu Sufyan chimed into the heated meeting taking place in the notorious Darun Nadwah. "They've been at war for as long as I can remember."

"Well, now, it doesn't matter how Muhammad accomplishes anything," said one of the chiefs. "What matters is how we respond."

Abu Jahl nodded briskly. "So are we just going to wait on the sidelines while Muhammad rises in power? In the name of Laat, OVER MY DEAD BODY!"

If there was one thing the Quraysh hated even more than the Muslims escaping Makkah, it was another city in Arabia challenging their position of power. Determined to destabilize Madinah in whichever way they could, they quickly summoned a scribe to write a document of their own—a threat that would surely convince the pagan Arabs to revolt against their new leader.

§

The Prophet had just finished advising a community member when someone burst into the mosque's courtyard. A frantic young man from the Ansar ran forward, skidding to a halt.

"Come quickly, O Messenger of Allah! The Quraysh have issued a threat to harm our families if you and your followers are not driven out!" Urgency laced his voice as he continued, "They sent word to all the tribe leaders to either expel or fight against you." He paused, sheepishly lowering his head. He didn't want to say what he had to say next. But he knew he had to.

"And...some of our leaders...are *already* rallying together a crowd!"

Someone gasped. The Prophet went out immediately to calm the situation. Though he appeared relaxed and unafraid, a band of his Companions stood up to join him. Flanked by Abu Bakr and Umar, a growing crowd followed him to the square, where a group of men was stoking the flames of division. A few Jewish men had emerged from their neighbourhoods upon hearing the commotion. They were standing on the side, assessing the situation in hushed tones, when they noticed the Prophet approaching.

His presence was enough to command everyone's attention. Prophet Muhammad addressed the crowd with a steady tone. Some of the troublemakers shuffled nervously while others naysaid whenever they could.

"We should have known this was too good to be true," one man mumbled, unaware that everyone could hear him loud and clear. He gulped and shifted behind another man to avoid Umar's piercing gaze.

"How can we be sure they won't attack us for not obeying them?" said another man, more bravely than he felt. His gaze darted between the murmuring onlookers and the still perfectly composed Prophet.

Abdullah Ibn Ubay— called Ibn Ubay, for short, was quick to give the commotion a further stir. "*Masha Allah*! Even *I* was thinking the same thing." He looked at the Prophet pointedly. "Are we expected to invite destruction upon our families?" His comrades stared at him, almost slack-jawed. One minute he's embracing Muhammad, commending him for making the Pact of Madina, and the next he's undermining him… They marvelled. He was clearly up to something.

Prophet Muhammad was deeply saddened by this. Abu Bakr noted how his tone did not change despite the disappointment on his face. The Prophet held firm, convincing the people not to give in to the scare tactics of the Quraysh. A hush fell over the crowd. Noticing the rebellious spark dying out, the Jewish spectators gradually disappeared, and those who rejoiced at this excuse to cause trouble left the square with their heads hung low. The Muslims watched as they tried in vain to hide their previously brandishing weapons in their robes.

Ibn Ubay was the last to leave. "I was only looking out for the community." He explained to the Prophet. "I'm sure you of all people understand why I reacted this way." He placed his hand over his chest, dipping his head to avoid eye contact, before parting with a resolute nod.

Soon, only the Prophet and his Companions remained standing together.

"So what will we do if the Quraysh come to attack us?" a young man asked nervously.

"We will be ready for them," was the confident reply from Umar, whose hand now gripped the handle of his sheathed sword.

If trouble did loom on the horizon, they intended to face it head-on.[6]

> *Faith (iman) must be expressed in practical terms. This was the first major lesson the Prophet taught his followers in Madinah. The building of the Masjid as a matter of urgency demonstrated that people must be committed to prayer. The policy of Brotherhood and Sisterhood meant that wealth had to be shared, and sacrificing for the community was part and parcel of being a true Believer. Finally, the Pact of Madinah shifted the spotlight away from tribalism and exploitation to values such as justice, fairness, and unity. These are the key ingredients for any community of Muslims—be that in the past or in the 21st century—to succeed in this life and the Afterlife.*

Chapter 3
Time To Strike Back

Resentment was at an all-time high in Makkah. Ever since the miraculous event that occurred in the Year of the Elephant, the Quraysh had been recognized as divinely protected leaders. They enjoyed the social status that came from being in charge of the Ka'bah and the hosts of the annual pilgrimage. However, the Prophet's successful escape, and their failure to create a revolt against him, had undermined that. They felt humiliated.

The Quraysh kept a close watch for any visitors from Madinah, intending full well to make an example of them. They were especially eager to loot what the emigrants had left behind and sent armed men to ransack their homes in broad daylight. The henchmen waved their swords, viciously threatening anyone who dared to intervene.

Among the crowd of murmuring onlookers stood a few Muslims. Unable to migrate due to sickness or lack of wealth, they had kept their faith hidden and hoped for the best. They watched helplessly as their relatives' belongings were thrown into a wagon, their homes emptied of any evidence that they ever existed.

"What are we going to do now?" a woman muttered just loud enough for her brother to hear.

"What *can* we do?" he said helplessly.

When the Muhajirun in Madinah found out they were furious. Not only were their properties burned to the ground, but their wealth was being loaded onto caravans to be sold off in Syria. In a show of arrogance, the Quraysh made sure to take the closest possible route to Madinah. They wanted everyone to see that as far as they were concerned, it was business as usual.

§

During this period, Islam successfully took root in the oasis. Unlike their Makkan counterparts, the Muslims in Madinah enjoyed the freedom to practice their faith. They recognized how blessed they were to perform the five daily prayers in congregation and looked forward to hearing the call to prayer given by Bilal. When the time arrived, footsteps would fill the sandy paths leading to the mosque to be led in prayer by Prophet Muhammad.

Revelation started coming down more often, declaring what was allowed and forbidden, and prescribing the obligatory acts of Islam, like giving charity (*zakat*) and fasting in the month of Ramadan. Prophet Muhammad diligently taught everything he'd received and strove to always be accessible to his followers or anyone who needed his advice. Despite effectively fostering a measure of coexistence between communities, there remained one pressing issue— the economy.

Since many of the Muhajirun had been made poor due to the migration and had lost all hope of reclaiming their property back in Makkah, the Prophet recognized the dire need to financially empower the Muslim community. He started contemplating the next steps required, and set off to learn more about the local markets. The practices he saw in and around the marketplaces of Madinah appalled him. It was not uncommon to hear someone complain in shock when it was time to pay.

"Have the prices gone up?!" an old man panicked, unaware that the merchant had sneakily added some extra weight to the scale to increase the price. In this way, many merchants overcharged, and in a show of generosity, would say: "No problem. Pay whatever you can now… and later on, you can pay me back what you owe."

But there was a catch, something the Prophet greatly disapproved of—adding interest (*riba*) on to the debt. Those who could not afford to pay in full were allowed to purchase the item, but on the condition that they paid a higher amount later. If they struggled to do so, a further charge was added as a penalty, which sent many spiralling into debt, pushing them deeper into poverty. The Muslims had no other choice but to participate in all this. And so, the old man would look at the merchant's outstretched hand and grudgingly part with his last silver coin in exchange for a sack of grain.

These injustices were also being witnessed in the Heavens. Revelation soon came down, openly warning against these practices:

Shame on the defrauders!

Those who take full measure when they buy from people, but give less than they should when they sell to others

Do such people not think that they will be resurrected on a tremendous Day—the Day all people will stand before the Lord of all worlds?

[Quran 83:1-7]

In light of these verses, the Prophet told the Muslims to avoid the marketplaces. He then set up a new marketplace known as Sook al-Manakha. It operated under two ground-breaking policies: the traders did not have to pay tax on their earnings, and the market would not be owned by any person or tribe, instead, it would be endowment belonging to all Muslims. With the banning of interest and other evil practices in the new market, customers felt confident that no one would take advantage of them. They carried their goods home with lighter steps, no longer burdened by the crushing weight of debt or late payment fees.

The other markets, owned and operated by Jewish tribes and pagans, noticed the sudden drop in customers. They were certainly not impressed. Meanwhile, Sook al-Manakha continued to thrive with a strong community spirit. Every morning it would spring to life as the merchants spread their goods out on makeshift tables. The no-tax policy attracted the attention of traders from even outside of Madinah.

A young Bedouin named Zahir loved visiting the new market and would often bring small goods from his village. One day, as he was carefully laying out neatly wrapped chunks of cottage cheese and butter, he sensed the presence of someone coming up behind him. His heart jolted when a pair of arms suddenly gripped his skinny waist, lifting his feet off the ground.

"W-who are you?! Put...me...down!" Zahir yelled, struggling to release himself from the person's firm grasp. "Put me down THIS INSTANT!"

Instead of answering him, the mysterious person called out, "Who will purchase this item?! Who will purchase this item?!" Zahir recognised the voice, he'd heard it plenty of times before and immediately stopped trying to wriggle free. *No wonder everyone looks so relaxed and jolly*, he told himself. Wearing a big smile of his own, he turned his head to the right to catch a glance, but the Prophet quickly moved his head to the left. Zahir turned to his left, and again the Prophet playfully shifted to the other side.

"O Messenger of Allah! Why would anyone part with their money for me?" he said, thinking of his unpleasant appearance and sweat-drenched clothes. "I'm not worth anything. No one would want me— even as a servant…" his voice trailed off.

Zahir was unhappy with how he looked. The Prophet was well aware of this, having noticed that the youth considered himself unattractive in the eyes of others. He loosened his grip, saying, "On the contrary, in the eyes of Allah, you are priceless!"

The Prophet's short but impactful words sliced through the young man's low self-esteem and gave him a whole new perspective. Zahir was overwhelmed. Blinking away tears, he leaned back into the Prophet's arms to hug him. The smell of musk coming from the Prophet's body made him close his eyes in happiness. The onlookers cheered at this beautiful encounter.

"*SubhanAllah*, the Prophet jokes like one of us!"

§

Despite the hustle and bustle of daily life, Prophet Muhammad still found time to visit his best friend Abu Bakr. Many things had changed since moving to Madinah, but their friendship remained as strong as ever. Their bond surpassed being old friends, for Abu Bakr was now Muhammad's father-in-law. Above all, Abu Bakr saw him as his Prophet and guiding light. They had just settled down for tea when the Prophet shared a verse of the Qur'an that had been revealed earlier that day.

Permission to fight back is now granted to those being fought as they have been wronged. And Allah is truly Most Capable of helping them succeed.
[Qur'an 22:39]

Abu Bakr quietly reflected on these words. With the recent act of aggression by the Quraysh, a confrontation was only a matter of time.[7] As long as their resentment persisted, war was inevitable. As the Prophet discussed his plan to create a united military force in preparation for what lay ahead, Abu Bakr wondered whether the Ansar would be willing to join them. Although they had sworn to fight if Madinah was under attack, going to war against the Quraysh outside the city was not something the Pledge of Aqabah had included. Both of them were acutely aware of this, but if Abu Bakr's past experiences had taught him anything, it was that as long as one assumed the best in people, they would respond accordingly...or so he hoped.

Many were, in fact, relieved by the permission to fight back—especially the Muhajirun. For years, the Prophet had instructed them to resist in only non-violent ways. Even in the face of harassment, torture, and the crippling boycott, they were not allowed to retaliate or fight back. Yet despite the distance of a desert between Makkah and Madinah, the tyranny of the Quraysh still seemed to reach them.

"Even though we no longer live there, they *still* find ways to wrong us," a woman from the Muhajirun had lamented as she sorted through a stash of barley, removing husks with deft hands. "Was it not enough for them to drive us out?"

Her younger friend let out a long sigh. "They act as though the things we left behind are theirs for the taking... like we left it there out of choice."

Her lips began to tremble as she glanced downwards. "I...I had left some things for my parents—they are poor, you see. I was hoping they could sell them and migrate to Madinah...but now I don't know if I'll ever see them again."

A woman from the Ansar took their hands in hers. "My sisters, Allah is their protector now." She looked them deep in their eyes and continued, "He takes care of His believing slaves. And He never burdens a soul more than it can bear."

"I pray and pray, but my heart is broken..." The young woman's eyes prickled with tears. "CURSE THOSE TYRANTS!" she snapped.

The Ansari woman rubbed her back to calm her. "Those tyrants you speak of may soon get what's coming to them," she remarked softly.

"Whatever do you mean?"

"Haven't you heard? The Prophet was given permission to fight back!"

The women stared, at first too stunned to speak, and then their faces lit up— *"Allahu Akbar!"*

Throughout the years, the Prophet had often wished more could be done to protect his followers as he witnessed the many times their patience had been stretched to breaking point. However, the command to take up armed resistance was a matter only Allah could decide. As soon as the new policy was revealed, he took swift action to shape the victimized community into an army fit to take on the mighty Quraysh.

During Friday sermons, he now spoke like the general of an army, his tone firm and direct. "We must prepare to meet the enemy with as much strength as possible." His voice filled the courtyard. His Companions hung onto every word that left his blessed lips as he encouraged them to practice archery and horsemanship. "Mark my words, there is strength in archery... strength is in archery...strength is in archery,"[8] he stressed.

Young and old came forward to train and join the army. Power, wealth, and fame had always motivated people to fight, but now they were drawn to a higher purpose, something bigger than themselves: to please Allah and protect His religion. The Prophet organized them into cavalry units and squadrons. Some were stationed on the outskirts of Madinah as the first line of defence, while the others scouted the surroundings to gather intelligence.

When the major trade months commenced, the Muslims became more alert. Spring and summer were especially busy times for the Quraysh, particularly en route to Syria. The Muslims were on their guard. The Prophet instructed his strongest horsemen to intercept the Makkan trade caravans, which potentially carried the Muhajirun's belongings. Eager to transform the stigma of exile into a banner of proud defiance, they mounted a pristine white flag on a lance and rode beneath it whenever they embarked on military expeditions.

However, these expeditions were surprisingly unsuccessful. Information about the caravans was not always accurate, and last-minute changes of plans were certainly not uncommon on these journeys. The cavalry units often returned home without so much as an encounter. Still, each expedition counted as training as it moulded their minds and strengthened their skills.

In March, almost a year after the migration, thirty Muhajirun under the command of the Prophet's uncle, Hamza, tried to intercept a caravan led by Abu Jahl.

Caught by surprise, the Quraysh chief swerved his horse when he saw the Muslim fighters heading their way. "Hold your positions," he commanded his men as he slunk to the back, darting towards a small village nearby. As a well-connected leader of the Makhzum Tribe, Abu Jahl had no trouble securing the help of a local Bedouin chieftain. He gave a haughty smirk as his ally obliged the Muslims to turn back empty-handed.[9]

A month later, the Muhajirun doubled their forces, this time approaching a caravan led by Abu Sufyan. They fired volleys of arrows to halt the caravan, but it was too heavily guarded for them to close in. And so, another caravan agonizingly slipped through their fingers.[10]

Prophet Muhammad decided to lead some of the military expeditions. Besides his experience on trade caravans as a merchant, he had also gained insight from his late wife Khadijah—a notable businesswoman in her own right. This gave him a unique perspective on the kind of arrangements made for the protection of caravans. Before heading out, he called for Sa'd ibn Ubadah.

The Companion arrived to see the Prophet readying his horse. "You sent for me, O Messenger of Allah?"

Despite being a noble chief from the Ansar, he did not expect the Prophet to appoint him to take charge of Madinah while he was away. "I will do my best to handle the city's affairs with excellence until you get back," promised Sa'd, the first Companion honoured with this role.

In September 623, the Prophet received a rather interesting report. A rich caravan was returning to Makkah, led by none other than Umayya, Bilal's former slave master and tormentor. It boasted around 2,500 camels carrying raisins, fine leather, and other attractive commodities. One hundred guards marched alongside this highly valuable caravan.

Anticipating that the Muhajirun's modest cavalry would struggle on their own against such a force, the Prophet assembled reinforcements. In no time, he was joined by 200 eager men, most of them of the Ansar. They marched out into the blazing sun and soon overtook the mountains, a majestic backdrop for the impending encounter. But when they reached their destination, there was no trace of the caravan.

"Where are they?" They scanned the horizon and inspected the sand for footprints.

"There's no sign of any passersby further out, let alone a large caravan," a returning scout informed them.

Abu Sufyan had caught wind of their plan and re-routed. But who informed him of our plan? The Prophet wondered.

"Follow me," the Prophet said, determined to make the most of the opportunity. He visited all the neighbouring villages to initiate peace treaties and share the message of Islam—something that would prove to be of strategic advantage later on.[11]

Three months later came news of another caravan headed by Abu Sufyan, though not as heavily guarded as before.

"About forty men are protecting it," the scout reported. "They're crossing the valley near the Red Sea."

Three-hundred Companions joined the Prophet on this expedition. They ventured off at full speed but, once again, arrived too late to stop the caravan. The men slid down the side of their horses, frustration evident on their faces. However, the Prophet did not see this as the end of the line. Knowing that the caravan would soon return from Syria, perhaps with even more goods, he dispatched two scouts to the coastal village of Hawra to keep an eye out for its return. Once there, they met a local chief who was willing to keep them hidden in his house for as long as they needed.

"We are blessed to be welcomed by such a generous host!"

"Indeed." The two conversed as they prepared to keep watch through the night. "Do you think we will manage to track down this caravan? We've not had much luck so far…"

"*Luck*! There's no such thing as luck my brother! Only the will of Allah."

"What do you mean?" The younger scout wrinkled his nose feeling slightly embarrassed.

"Whatever Allah decrees comes to pass… and whatever He doesn't will never happen. I heard the Prophet say as much. Luck has nothing to do with it."

"I see," he said with a nod, then added, "Now that I think of it, the Messenger of Allah seemed very optimistic that Abu

Sufyan *would* return with a greater load—*insha Allah*, we will not fail in our mission."

The scouts slept in turns, remaining on high alert as the days went by. Neither the calming scenery nor the cool sea breeze could distract them from their duty. As soon as they noticed Abu Sufyan's caravan entering the village, they galloped back to Madinah with the news.

The Prophet recruited 313 men to intercept the caravan. The objective: seize the goods being transported and take back what was rightfully theirs. They headed for Badr, a place 150 kilometres southwest near the Red Sea, where a large valley opened out into the coastal flatland. Several wells had been dug into its sides and cisterns had been hollowed out to hold the residue of winter flash floods. This place was thus a major resting spot, and never more so than when Makkah's big spring caravan stopped there on its way back from Syria.

The Muslims were counting on the Quraysh to stick to their old habits, and since it was not meant to be an all-out battle, they took only light weaponry, two horses, and seventy camels, taking turns to ride them on their way.

The valley of Badr, surrounded by two great dunes, laid beneath the bare slopes of a mountain. There, victory and defeat would be woven into the fabric of history, and the sands would welcome the fallen heroes and villains in what would be known as the greatest battle in Muslim history.

Those who choose disbelief over belief and rebel against the command of Allah and the Prophet ﷺ often think they can outwit the people of the truth. They are confident that their plans will always be successful. They rely wholeheartedly on their abilities and resources. They can even reach the point of delusion, whereby their scheming and plotting are clearly paving the way to their own downfall—but they fail to see that this is a form of Divine Punishment. This is why the great Companion Umar would pray, "O Allah, enable us to see the truth as the truth and to follow it. And enable us to see falsehood as falsehood and stay away from it."

Chapter 4
An Unexpected Encounter

A still quiet filled the dusty alleyways as darkness cloaked Makkah. All slept peacefully, except for the Prophet's aunt Atikah, whose dream left her feeling like a catastrophe was about to unfold.

She woke up with a gasp, "get my brother!" she called out, clutching fistfuls of the shawl draped over her shivering body. A servant poked his head in the room, puzzled by the urgency in her voice. Atikah shuffled forward, waving her hand as she cried, "Send for Abbas, QUICKLY!"

Abbas had barely set foot in the house when his sister ran to him, hands clasped and eyebrows knitted in agitation. He was almost afraid to ask what had happened. "Atikah! Whatever is the matter?"

"O Abbas! It was terrifying!" she said, shaking her head. "I saw a man racing on a camel to Makkah. He stopped when he reached a valley and called out to a group of people saying, 'O men who betray traditions, come forward and receive a disaster that in three days shall crush you.'"

She closed her eyes, still breathing heavily, recalling the dream.

"Go on. What next?"

"Then I saw people gathering around him, following him as he entered a sanctuary. His camel carried him to the top of the Ka'bah, where he repeated his call, and then it bolted to the top of a nearby mountain. Again, he cried out to the people with the same message. Then he bent down and picked up an enormous boulder, which he launched into the air— if only you could have seen it! It exploded into countless pieces, each one striking a target inside the city." She took a shuddering breath. "There wasn't a single home in Makkah that was spared."[12]

"Now, calm down, my dear sister," he said, placing his hand on her shoulder. "Let's think about this before rushing to conclusions…"

Abbas' initial thought was to dismiss the whole thing as a weird nightmare, but the more he thought about the dream, the more alarming it seemed. Deep in his bones, he felt that something momentous was going to happen.

"Look," he was staring at her now, his gaze heavy and uncomfortable. "This does *seem* to be a dangerous sign," he admitted. "But I'm worried that if you tell anyone about it, it could get us all into a lot of trouble. So keep it to yourself. Don't say a word."

Despite being so insistent with his sister, he was unable to follow his own advice. Later that day, he met with his good friend Walid and ended up telling him all about it, making sure to add, "O Walid! Please don't tell anyone else." Though Walid swore on the gods, he recounted the dream to his father, saying, "Don't tell anyone." Walid's father, Utbah, loved to gossip and couldn't resist sharing the story. Soon enough, the news spread throughout Makkah, passing from person to person, accompanied by the irresistible phrase— "Don't tell anyone!"

When it reached Abu Jahl, the crooked chief wasted no time in confronting Abbas. Like a beast lying in wait, he stood in the shade of the Ka'bah, waiting for the Prophet's uncle to pass by at his usual time. When Abu Jahl sighted his target, a smile slithered onto his face. He spoke loud enough for others to hear,

"O sons of Abdul Muttalib, how long has your prophetess been uttering her pearls of wisdom?"

"Wh…what do you mean?" Abbas pretended to be clueless.

"I'm referring to your sister's…*vision*." Abu Jahl drawled. "Is it not enough that your men pretend to be prophets?"

Abbas blinked, taken aback by this barrage of insults against not only his sister and nephew Muhammad, but his *entire* family. Abu Jahl shook his head in disappointment and started walking away. With his robe draping behind him, he whispered in Abbas' ear as he strolled past, "I hope for your sake something does happen in three days' time…"

§

Like Prophet Muhammad, Abu Sufyan also had scouts on the lookout, but they were operating from within the heart of the Muslim community. Hypocrites—which is the only way to describe them—sent word to Abu Sufyan the very moment Prophet Muhammad had dispatched the two scouts to Hawra. When he learned of the Muslims' presence, he panicked and sent word to Makkah, urging them to raise an army to come to the rescue. In the meantime, he ordered his men to press forward on a more secretive coastal route, travelling by both day and night.

When Abu Sufyan's messenger entered the city, he sped to the Ka'bah to make a public announcement. Abu Jahl looked like he had seen a ghost. He slunk into the shadow of the nearest altar, avoiding eye contact with Abbas, who was sitting at the Ka'bah waiting for precisely this moment to arrive. Three days had now passed.

Abu Sufyan had given specific instructions to Damdam to make his entrance as dramatic as possible, so the man had slit his camel's nose, blood spurting all over as he rode in, and was sitting backwards on the saddle. The spectacle certainly grabbed everyone's attention. Children shrieked. A woman dropped a bucket of water she had drawn from the well. People stopped their activities and swarmed to the Ka'bah.

Damdam shouted, "O people! Come forward! Be quick!" He cupped his hands around his mouth to amplify his voice. "Your wealth is being attacked by Muhammad and his followers as we speak! You won't be able to defend it unless you act immediately!"

So this was the man on the camel making the announcements in my sister's dream… Abbas became wide-eyed at the realization.

The crowd erupted— shouting, wailing, and clamouring for something to be done. Though people sensed Damdam might've been exaggerating, their nerves were on edge. This caravan held one of their richest loads yet, and the idea of losing it made them very uncomfortable.

Abu Jahl watched the panic unfolding before him. His mind travelled back in time to when they used to mock Muhammad at the Ka'bah. The memory played out in front of him as clear as day. He remembered the hurt flickering in the Prophet's eyes that fateful day when he had driven him to supplicate against them.

Regret struck Abu Jahl. But only for a moment. He squashed the feeling and stomped off, barging people out of his way, well aware of the narrowed eyes following his departure.

§

The door swung open into a large stoned hallway. Abu Lahab squinted up at the tall, black-haired man fuming at the entrance; the scar that pulled downwards on his right cheek made his expression even sterner.

More bad news, I suppose, Abu Lahab thought, sighing in frustration. *I guess lunch will have to wait.*

"Your nephew continues to make trouble for us," said Abu Jahl, straightening his emerald green robe.

"I've told you before, do NOT refer to him as my nephew!"

Abu Jahl continued dismissively, "Just listen to me. Abu Sufyan's caravan barely managed to slip past him heading up to Syria, but a message has now reached us that Muhammad has not given up. He's going to try and ambush them on their way back."

"He was always very persistent, wasn't he?" Abu Lahab frowned. "I thought our friend in Yathrib was *handling* things for us." — like many leaders of the Quraysh, he refused to acknowledge the city's new name.

"It doesn't seem like it." Abu Jahl scowled. "Almost half our wealth is on the backs of those camels!"

The two exchanged worried looks as Abu Lahab pulled the door open wider. "This conversation is going to take up my whole day," he muttered under his breath as he let his fellow chief in.

After Abu Talib's death, Abu Lahab became chief of the Hashim Tribe. To complement his new role, he had built for himself the biggest house in Makkah. The entrance hall alone was wide enough to fit a large camel. Light poured in from the arched windows cut into thick stone walls. The pair walked past the rows of unlit torches lining the hallway and up a magnificent marble staircase that led to an open-roof balcony overlooking the Ka'bah.

The other chiefs of Makkah were quickly summoned to join them. War was on the agenda. By the end of the meeting, Abu Jahl was appointed as army general. Abu Lahab beckoned a servant with a wave of his hand, sending him to find the strongest man who owed him a favour.

"What for? Aren't you joining us?" asked Abu Jahl, quirking an eyebrow.

"I will send a warrior on my behalf." Abu Lahab replied with a reassuring nod. "My health does not permit me! My belly alone would need a horse!" he said, patting his protruding stomach.

Abu Jahl barked a laugh. "You stay put old friend. I will teach them a lesson once and for all." He reached for his sword, grinning wickedly. Abu Lahab chuckled and wished his comrade well, blissfully unaware that neither of them would be smiling if they knew what awaited them.

§

The noonday sun seared the golden expanse of the desert. The Companions had paused to give their riding animals a much-needed break at a nearby oasis a few miles from Badr. A group of men were scattered around to keep watch while the rest sipped water, some unwrapping their turbans to fan themselves. They were about to resume their march when a figure in the distance came galloping towards them. The man jumped off his camel, lowering his face covering to reveal his identity. He greeted the Prophet before sharing the news.

"The Quraysh have raised an army to defend Abu Sufyan's caravan."

Some of the youngsters stiffened slightly at this. Everyone within earshot stopped what they were doing, coming closer to listen.

"Some Bedouins witnessed their approach. From what we gather, many tribes have joined, and they could be in the hundreds, maybe more! Only Allah knows."

The Prophet noticed the expressions on peoples' faces as a degree of apprehension filled the dry air. The situation had gone from confiscating a weakly protected caravan to the possibility of a full-scale battle— something they had not prepared for when they left Madinah. With the prospect of war now an imminent reality, he consulted his Companions on whether they should proceed or retreat.

Abu Bakr was the first to assure the Prophet of his unconditional support. Umar agreed and voiced the Muhajirun's willingness to proceed. They too added some words of support which touched the Prophet; not that he was surprised, for he knew that the emigrants from Makkah were unreservedly with him. But could the same be said of the Ansar who were present? They had gathered for the purpose of capturing the caravan, but now something far more dangerous was facing them, something that was not part of the Pledge of Aqabah.

Would they be prepared to help me against an enemy now that I'm no longer in Madinah? The Prophet wondered, knowing there was only one way to find out. However, he did not want to use his position and reputation to burden them with more than they had agreed to do. And yet, he was fully aware that if the Ansar opted out, their already modest army would shrink dramatically, leaving him and the Muhajirun in a dangerous position. For them to stand a chance against the mighty army of the Quraysh, they *had* to stick together.

"The rest of you, let me hear your thoughts too," the Prophet said, looking over at the Ansar as he spoke. By now, they had already sensed that they were the reason for his concern, and so Sa'd the son of Muadh, being a notable chief from the Aws Tribe, stepped forward.

"It would seem, O Messenger of Allah, that you wish for us to speak?"

The Prophet nodded and gestured for him to speak his mind.

"Know this…" Sa'd placed his hand on his chest, "we believe in you and are convinced of what you have told us. We testify that your message is the truth. We have sworn allegiance to hear and obey." He then pointed in the direction of the Red Sea. "I swear by the One who sent you with the truth, if you were to head into the middle of the ocean, we would march right behind you. Even if it meant drowning in the process. I assure you…not a single one of us would turn back!"

His words stirred the emotions of the Ansar, who shot up to echo the sentiment, punching their fists skywards and nodding.

"We are well-trained in the art of war," Sa'd continued, his words flowing even more effortlessly. "Perhaps Allah will bring coolness to your eyes when you witness our talents. So lead us into the battlefield, in the Name of Allah!"

The Prophet's face lit up at his words, and the tension in his shoulders began to ease. His Companions' commitment to look out for each other on the battlefield filled him with warmth. The impressive speech had certainly boosted their morale; it showed in the way they readied themselves to continue their march.

The Prophet took charge. "Onwards," he said, his voice strong with certainty. "I bring you good news from Allah. He has promised me either the riches from the caravan or victory on the battlefield. By Allah, there is a vision before me of a battlefield, and I see the exact places where each of our enemies will fall."

And so they marched on, arriving at Badr later that day with the unshakable feeling that they were not the first to have reached the valley.

§

17 March AD 623

The Muslims set up camp well before the evening deepened. As soon as night fell, the Prophet sent scouts to the nearby wells. They spread out into the darkened valley, treading carefully into the thick of silence. The splatter of stars provided barely enough light to navigate the uneven terrain. A rustling sound caught their attention.

"Look. There, near the well," one of the scouts whispered excitedly to his comrade.

"Ah yes. I see them."

Two young men were loading up containers of water to their camels. The scouts studied their behaviour for a while.

"There's no sign of an army nearby. I'm sure they're with Abu Sufyan."

"They must be. Let's go!"

They swiftly overpowered the men and brought them back to camp. Prophet Muhammad was busy praying when they arrived. The adrenaline still rushing through their veins made them start the integration without him.

"Who are you? And who are you with?" They asked, repeating the questions in a harsher tone when the pair refused to answer.

"Look, friends. You can either tell me who you're with," one of the men said slowly, "or I'll let this one speak to you *with his fists…*"

"We're with Abu Jahl and his army," they finally admitted. "Don't kill us— please!"

"Be honest! You're with Abu Sufyan, *aren't you?*"

"No, we are not!" they insisted.

"Where is Abu Sufyan now?"

"We don't know!"

Deep down, the scouts still hoped that they would be able to seize the caravan as originally planned. They so badly wanted these two to be Abu Sufyan's men that when they didn't get the answers they wanted, they resorted to beating them.

"Stop!" the captives cried at last. "We confess! We *are* with Abu Sufyan's caravan!"

Just then, the Prophet finished his prayer. He got up and walked purposefully towards the scouts with a serious expression. "When they told you the truth, you beat them, and when they lied, you let them be," he admonished. He then glanced at the two snivelling captives. "Indeed, they are from the army of the Quraysh. Aren't you?"

The pair of them looked up as one. The Prophet had a warm face and kind eyes, which made a calmness settle over them. He squatted down, coming to eye level with them. "Tell me about the Quraysh, about their whereabouts," he said without urging them to answer.

The older of the two tilted his head in one direction. "They are behind that mountain."

"Yes, on the far side of the valley," the other man added.

The Prophet nodded. "And how many men are they?"

"A great many, and they are heavily armed," they revealed. The Prophet asked again about their numbers, this time more serious in tone, but the men became tight-lipped, giving only vague answers. The Prophet then asked a seemingly unrelated question, "And how many animals do they slaughter each day?"

"One day nine, the next day ten…" the youngest replied slowly, scrunching his face as he wondered how that information could be useful. What the Prophet said next surprised everyone.

"Then they must be between nine hundred and a thousand," he concluded, "since one camel can feed a hundred men."

Everyone close enough to hear this exchanged nervous glances. Even though the Prophet's calculation was impressive, the information itself unsettled them— if this was true, it meant they would be significantly outnumbered by their opponents. Three-to-one! The army of the Quraysh was also equipped with 100 horses—compared to the two the Muslims had—as well as 500 camels. It was the largest army ever gathered by the people of Makkah.

The Prophet asked his final question, "Which of the leaders of Quraysh is present?" The captives mentioned fifteen senior chiefs, including Umayya, Utbah, and Abu Jahl. The Prophet returned to his tent, unperturbed, saying, "The Quraysh have flung their dearest flesh and blood to you O Muslims."[13]

The Prophet instructed his men to shift their location to higher ground, and then to swiftly block up the wells and cisterns closest to the Quraysh so that at dawn they'd be forced to fight from a position more favourable to the Muslims. By controlling access to the water, he would control the battlefield.

That night, the Prophet stayed awake while the others rested. Ali was stationed as a watchman and could see his dear cousin sitting beneath a nearby tree engaged in worship. The cool drizzle of rain created a calmness in the camp as the men slept. The Prophet prayed with all his heart and every ounce of energy he could muster. Before the morning sun rose, the Muslims offered their first prayer of the day in congregation. After this, the Prophet once again entered a state of worship.

Facing the direction of Makkah, he raised his hands high towards the sky and called out to his Lord, "O Allah, here are the Quraysh! They have come in reckless pomp and arrogance, opposing You and calling me a liar. My Lord, grant me Your help which You have promised! Please, My Lord, grant us Your promise, because if this small group of believers is destroyed, there will be no one left to worship You."

At one point, he raised his hands so high that his cloak fell to the ground. Abu Bakr rushed over to pull it back up. When he heard what the Prophet was saying, he realized how severely the situation was affecting him. Abu Bakr's eyes welled up with tears. He hugged his dear friend from behind, pulling him into a tight embrace. "Enough, O Messenger of Allah," he said gently, almost beseechingly. "You have made all the prayers you possibly can. Allah will surely deliver us the victory He has promised."[14]

Chapter 5
A Miraculous Victory

Scrawling sounds filled the air as a strong gust of wind hurled grains of sand upwards, creating a veil between the Muslim ranks and the enemy. The valley of Badr between them was bare, broken up by the occasional shrub and scatter of pebbles. The rain from the night before had made the sand remarkably even and smooth closer to the Muslims' side. Vultures circled overhead, settling on boulders behind the two armies, like hungry spectators anticipating a feast.

When the dust settled, the Prophet's men could see the army in the distance. Horses and camels filled rank after rank, accompanied by heavily equipped men, ready for war. The Muslims stood steady, spears to their sides and shields on their backs. Hamza stepped forward with a determined look, openly watching the opponents as he gripped his trusty sword. He made for a striking image; a single, elegant ostrich feather decorated his chest armour compared to the full-on war regalia worn by the leaders of the Quraysh.

The Quraysh forces looked fierce, their weapons gleaming menacingly in the sunlight. Abu Jahl had organized them well. Shortspears in the front ranks, longspears and javelins next, archers at the sides. However, the number of soldiers seemed surprisingly low compared to the reports the Muslims had received.

"Is that all of them?" the Companion, Ibn Masud, asked his comrade. They watched as the remaining enemy troops advanced from behind the hill on the far side of the valley. The army appeared fewer than they truly were—a Divine intervention of Allah meant to boost the morale of the modestly equipped Muslim army.

"They don't look more than…what, a hundred?"

"I agree. Perhaps closer to seventy…"

"*Allahu Akbar!*" The young comrade cheered. "We were worried for no reason."[15]

Their expressions eased as their confidence grew. However, the relief was not shared by all. Several Muslim soldiers raised their hands, shielding their eyes from the morning sunrays as they scanned the enemy ranks, hoping that among the familiar faces, they would not find a family member present. Abu Bakr's eyes were drawn to a particular young man on the front lines. Only his eyes were visible through the slit of his face guard, yet Abu Bakr immediately recognized him. His heart plummeted. *My son.*

Meanwhile, on the opposite end, an elder reassured Abu Bakr's son, Abdur Rahman, that he was doing the right thing. The men encouraged each other by boasting about their unmatched cavalry and the hardened war veterans on their side. However, not everyone was eager to fight.

Utbah had a sudden change of heart when he saw his son on the other side. He trotted forward on his red camel and turned to face a group of soldiers. "By God, if you defeat Muhammad in battle, you will not be able to look one another in the face without feeling disgust, for you will be looking at someone who has killed *your* nephew or *your* relative…" He paused a while to let his words sink in. "Come! Let us turn back."

The men exchanged uneasy glances, wavering for just a moment before Abu Jahl showed up on horseback with a gaze as sharp as his sword. He had been watching Utbah give his speech with seething fury. The same fury he had felt when he heard Suraaqa the assassin had converted to Islam at the hands of the Prophet during his migration.

"You pathetic coward!" he said, waving his sword in Utbah's face.

"My noble comrade," Utbah said, raising his hands as if to deflect the animosity radiating off his fellow chief. "I'm a fearless man, and if we kill Muhammad, then true, we will all gain what we desire, but if we turn back, we will look noble for showing restraint and mercy."

"Your lungs are inflated with fear." Abu Jahl sneered. With a withering smirk, he steered his horse to show its backside to Utbah, turning to face another notable of the Quraysh. Amir's brother had been killed trying to protect a caravan from the Muslim cavalry not too long ago. Abu Jahl eyed the man knowingly and said, "The blood of your brother is not yet dry, and you wish to turn back on his killers? They murdered him in cold blood just one moon ago— *one moon.*"

Everyone looked to see how Amir would react. Abu Jahl's mouth almost cracked into a wicked grin when the man's brow crinkled, his face crumpling with emotion. Amir jumped off his horse and, in a fit of grief, began pulling off his armour piece by piece as he lamented, "My brother! My brother! MY DEAR BROTHER!"

This emotional display reignited the mood for battle.

"Now. Be ready to fight! Make them pay. Fight and kill!" Abu Jahl said to the soldiers, giving Utbah a pointed look. The older man looked downwards, effectively humiliated by his comrade's manipulative tactics. The passion for war now burned more intensely than ever.

Abu Jahl watched the small force on the opposite end of the valley. "They are no match for us. We will crush them— in the name of Uzza, and the legacy of our forefathers! This war will be over before the sun is set," he declared. The Quraysh would not turn back. Not when victory was being handed to them on a silver platter.

Over in the Muslim camp, the Prophet, clad in armour, walked row by row as he arranged his army. He straightened their formation, pointing with the arrow in his hand. "Stand in line, O Sawad," he said to one of the Ansar who stood a little ahead of his rank, lightly prodding him in the chest for good measure.

"That hurt," Sawad complained. The Prophet stopped in his tracks. "O Messenger of Allah, Allah has sent you with truth *and* justice, so allow me to retaliate."

His boldness startled those within earshot. They were even more surprised when the Prophet handed the arrow over to Sawad. "You may retaliate," he said, spreading his arms wide open to expose his chest.

The Companions watched in astonishment as Sawad stepped forward; but instead of poking the Prophet, he placed his cheek against his chest. When asked why he did so, he replied, "O Messenger of Allah, given what awaits us, it's possible that I may not live to see another day. And if this truly is my final moments in this world, I wish for it to be spent close to you."[16]

Prophet Muhammad smiled warmly, then blessed him and prayed for him. People smiled in admiration; the heart-warming moment sliced through the tension of the impending battle. After examining the ranks, the Prophet went to a structure made from palm trees, where his closest Companions joined him to finalize their strategy.

§

The SIMPLE SEERAH - PART TWO

After Abu Jahl's verbal onslaught, Utbah felt humiliation simmering in his core. It was pushing him to act. To prove himself. To fight.

Taking a deep breath, he grabbed his sword, waving it high as he galloped forward in full sight of both armies. Battles in Arabia traditionally began with one-to-one duels, so Utbah put himself forward for this position. His honour demanded it. His brother and son, Shaybah and Walid, joined him for the sake of their family's honour. They stopped close to the Muslim army and slid off their mounts.

"Who will come and face us? Three against three," they said, showing off their armour.

The Prophet looked to men from his own family to respond to the challenge of a duel.

"Step forward, O Ubaydah," he called his older cousin, a bastion of bravery. He responded immediately.

"Step forward, O Hamza!" The warrior renowned for hunting lions came to stand alongside him.

"Step forward, O Ali." The young boy who was one of the first to support the Prophet had grown into a fine young man, well-trained in combat. He too, came forward.

The three marched forward to meet their opponents on the battleground. Ubaydah, being the oldest and most experienced, stood before Utbah. Hamza met Shaybah's glare with a hardened gaze of his own while Ali faced Walid. The men circled one another, their eyes trained on their respective opponents as they unsheathed their swords. Everyone looked on in suspense, and then metal met metal with a resounding clang.

The duels were brief and deadly.

Hamza and Ali were soon standing over the cinder-eyed corpses of Shaybah and Walid. Ubaydah found himself locked in battle with Utbah, who seemed to be gaining the upper hand. He ducked and spun around, managing to strike Utbah with a powerful blow that sent him crashing to the ground. When Abu Bakr saw this, he sighed with relief, recalling the beating he'd received at the hands of the Makkan leader over a decade ago.

Utbah still had fight left in him. He rolled to the side and leapt to his feet, only to receive another blow, even more powerful than the first. This time he managed to catch it with his shield. The air rang with the resounding clang of carapace against steel. The force made him bend beneath the blow, going down on one knee. He felt his breath on his chest as Ubaydah thrusted his weight behind it, pushing him further down. Just when it seemed as though Utbah was about to collapse under the pressure, he managed to pull out a dagger tucked inside his boot and violently swung it at Ubaydah's thigh while falling back.

The dagger cut deep, sending Ubaydah to the ground. Hamza and Ali sprinted over to finish Utbah, before tending to him. Ubaydah grunted as they carried him back. Even as a river of blood gushed out from his leg, there was only one thought on his mind.

"Am I…not…a martyr, O Messenger of Allah?" he said between gasps when the Prophet rushed over to him.

"Indeed you are," he replied firmly, his eyes glimmering with emotion as he took hold of his cousin's hand. The other soldiers nearby nodded reassuringly as they tried their best to tend to him. Too weak to say anything else, Ubaydah gave the Prophet's hand a firm squeeze before taking his last breath.

§

The battle was now poised to begin. An arrow from the enemy's side hissed through the air and a soldier from the Ansar dropped to the ground with a fatal wound. Another arrow followed, striking Haritha, a young man from the Ansar who had been drinking at one of the wells. His blood sprayed across the golden sand.

Steadying his horse, Abu Bakr looked to the Prophet for a command, a signal for their army to attack, but he was motionless, staring down at his cousin. Hundreds of arrows split through the sky, dimming the sun as they arched and rained down into the shields held up by the Muslims. Sensing that something wasn't right, Abu Bakr passed the reins to the nearest soldier and rushed over. He peered into the Messenger's black eyes and saw them glance upwards as he passed out, slumping into his arms.

Abu Bakr's breath caught in his throat. Much to his relief, the Prophet's eyes snapped open a moment later.

The Prophet gathered his strength and stood upright, facing the Makkan army. Abu Bakr watched him curiously as he picked up a handful of sand and threw it in the enemy's direction, saying, "May confusion seize them!"

A powerful wind rose from behind the Messenger, rustling the canvas of the tents and fluttering his cloak. It surged forward, drowning out the relentless blasting of the enemy's horns. A blinding sand cloud then swept across the plain and swallowed the Quraysh, prickles of sand stinging their faces.

Abu Bakr watched in amazement as Prophet Muhammad called on his men. It was hard to believe that he had passed out just a moment ago. The Prophet's gaze shone with unshakable determination as he spoke. "By the One in whose Hand rests my soul, every man who fights them bravely and advances without retreating will have Allah grant him entry into Paradise."

His words rippled through the ranks. Soldiers carried the message to those out of earshot. A soldier from the Ansar named Umayr threw the dates he had been snacking on over his shoulder. "By Allah!" he cried. "The only thing stopping me from entering Paradise right now are these dates!" He gripped his sword, ready for battle.

The sun blazed reddish-white on the horizon, lighting the wispy clouds with a spray of colour, like paint thrown on a canvas. In the backdrop of both armies was an endless flow of dunes, silent witnesses of history in the making. On the Prophet's command, the Muslims charged forward, weapons in hand and faith in their hearts. "*Ahad! Ahad!*" they chanted, glorifying Allah's Oneness.

Soldiers on the Quraysh side scoffed as the entire army started moving in a clamour of marching boots. Their neat lines soon disintegrated as soldiers broke into a chaotic dash towards the Muslims, swinging their heavy swords. The two armies collided in a flurry of battle cries. Fierce fighting broke out. Sounds of clashing swords and slamming shields filled the valley. The Muslims were vastly outnumbered but kept to the battle formations the Prophet had instructed. Archers fired from the rear while front-line fighters kept the enemy at bay with their spears. Though ill-equipped, they held their ground.

A young man from the Ansar groaned when an opponent stepped on his hand, crushing it with a cruel smile. "So where's your god now?" grunted the soldier as he hoisted the youngster into the air, high enough for his legs to dangle. If he thought he would reduce the youth to tears, he was badly mistaken. He screamed as something sharp was plunged into his neck. The youth had acted quickly, using his free hand to grab an arrow from his quiver. He rolled away the moment he landed on the ground, disappearing behind the shield of a nearby comrade.

The Prophet fought alongside his men, and when the battle would intensify, those closest to him would fall behind in V-shaped formation, as he spearheaded their charge. They engaged only enemy squads that got too close, and didn't chase down stragglers. The strategy was shaped through months of tireless training, and it was working. At one point, the Prophet turned to his best friend, smiling as he said, "O Abu Bakr! Glad tidings to you. Allah's victory is approaching. I swear by Allah, I can see the Angel Jibril on horseback emerging from a sandstorm."

It happened suddenly. No sooner had he said that than the neighing of horses bellowed from behind the rocky hills. Support from the Heavens came from the right and left. Thousands of Allah's select angels swooped down from the sky on the backs of piebald horses that raced across the sand, their hooves barely skimming the ground.

The invisible soldiers fought alongside the Muslim army. Although their presence was felt by all, only a select few caught brief glimpses of the angels. To some, they appeared like the warping of air, as if the wind itself had become visible. Their steeds galloped, leaving a trail of slain Makkan fighters with signature burn marks over their necks, fingers, and toes. Together with their human comrades, they overwhelmed the enemy.

For most of the battle, Abu Jahl had had his strongest men at his side as they loudly tallied up their victims. Now, he stood on his own as a troop of massive horses galloped towards him, each bearing a rider in gleaming armour that seemed to radiate light and had no chain underneath it. Each figure carried a sword in one hand, as long as a man was tall.

Can this really be happening? Abu Jahl thought with mounting terror. His heart began pounding like a frightened animal in his chest, his legs no longer steady; at least not enough to run away. *I should have never disbelieved in the God of Muhammad,* he admitted to himself, collapsing onto his knees just as the figures charged into him.

The war cries of the Quraysh turned to silence upon seeing their leader lying motionless on the ground. They stood in a petrified daze— as if their faces had been plunged into water— trying to come to terms with the drastic change of events. Turning on their heels, they ditched their armour and animals, and anything else that would slow them down.

A trail of scattered swords and bent spears was left in their wake. At least seventy men from the Quraysh had been killed, including many leaders. A similar number of men failed to get away and were taken as prisoners as the battle sounds came to an end.

§

What the runaways did not know was that their bloodthirsty chief had survived. Abu Jahl was not yet dead, for the angels had chosen *not* to finish him off. When he came to, he still had enough life in him to recognize the man approaching him.

Ibn Masud had had the honour of being the first to recite the Qur'an in front of the Ka'bah. Since he was not born into wealth or the protection of a famous tribe, Abu Jahl had seized the opportunity in Makkah to humiliate him for being so daring. The vicious leader of the Makhzum Tribe had struck him with a severe blow to the face, hostility burning in his dark eyes. Ibn Masud found that same venomous look directed at him now as he stood over the snarling chief. He placed his foot on Abu Jahl's neck, the Muslims' most ardent oppressor now beneath him in more ways than one.

"You...you certainly have climbed high in life, little shepherd," Abu Jahl spat between breaths.

"A shepherd maybe, but smart enough to recognize the truth"

"Tell me... which way did fortune swing in the end?"

"Allah and His Messenger have won," Ibn Masud answered bluntly. "Not because of *luck*. Because Islam is the truth."

"You think I'm evil, don't you?" Abu Jahl's words were now barely audible. Ibn Masud relaxed his foot to allow him to speak more freely. "...All I wanted was to honour our forefathers and protect our traditions."

"Even *after* it became clear that was all wrong?"

Abu Jahl's eyes flashed. "I'm never wrong, you fool."

Ibn Masud had heard enough. This man was never going to change. Even in the throes of death, his arrogance persisted. With a quick motion of his sword, Ibn Masud ended the reign of terror that was Abu Jahl, a man so despicable, he didn't deserve to have his life taken by angels. The Prophet would later describe him as the Pharaoh of this nation.

When it became clear the Quraysh would not be returning, the Prophet called Zayd, the former slave who was like a son to him. He gave him his own camel, Qaswa, saying, "Share the good news of our victory with the people of Madinah."

When Zayd entered the city, the people recognized the Prophet's camel and rushed out to hear what had happened. He wore the news on his face. As soon as they saw his expression, they broke into cheers. *"Allahu Akbar!"* Everyone listened in wonder as Zayd listed the names of those who had been slain— nearly every notorious figure of the Quraysh. Some naysayers tried to dismiss the story, but there was Qaswa, peacefully munching on dried grass, an undeniable sign that Zayd was telling the truth.

After the battle, the Muslim army got to work, tending to the wounded and completing various tasks before nightfall. A group of men freshening up at the wells greeted the Prophet as he walked by that evening. The Prophet wore a sombre expression as he came to a stand at the ditch which held the bodies of the enemies.

"O men inside this ditch, tribesmen of your Prophet," he began, "how terrible was the care you showed me..." he sighed, a mixture of frustration and pity. "You called me a liar when people from outside believed in me. You fought against me when others helped me to victory. Have you found the promise of punishment from your Lord to be true? Because I have found His promise of reward to be true."

Some of his Companions overheard him and found this conversation with the dead odd. "Do you know they can hear me just like you can right now?" the Prophet explained, "except that they cannot reply to me."[17] He gave one last glance into the ditch and turned around to join his Companions, the people whose love and loyalty felt like that of family.

It wasn't long before tales of angels on spotted horses soaked the Arabian Peninsula. The Battle of Badr would go down in history as a turning point, and the Companions who defended Islam in its first and most decisive battle would forever be held in high esteem.

The Battle of Badr was fought on March 17, 624, and though it was not quite what the Prophet had sought, it would turn out to be exactly what the Muslims needed. What happened that day was a timeless example that strength does not lie in weapons and numbers. Although the odds were stacked against them, they were armed with the most important weapon of all: faith (iman). This is then a reminder to all Muslims today, that the most precious gift they have is their faith. Only by protecting and nurturing it will they earn the support of Allah, which they greatly desire in times of need.

Chapter 6
A New Reality

"It *can't* be true!"

At first, no one could believe it. How could almost all of their leaders have been killed? And seventy of their men be captured? Bewildered and enraged, the people of Makkah struggled to accept their army's crushing defeat. However, the absence of their fallen leaders spoke for itself, and the downcast expressions of the soldiers trickling into the city removed any shred of doubt.

A particularly sullen soldier trudged towards the Ka'bah with his head hung low after sharing his account of the battle with some people. A slurred voice interrupted his thoughts. He looked up to see Abu Lahab waving him over. The thickset man had been resting in the shade of the Ka'bah with a bowl of grapes and a jug of wine. "Come, come here and tell me everything that happened!" he said, patting the plush cushion beside him.

The young man sat down. He cringed, recounting the jarring battle. "We faced the enemy, confident we would win. In the beginning, they appeared few in number, but as the battle went on, they seemed to multiply!" He shook his head in disbelief. "More and more of them kept appearing!" Abu Lahab paused mid-gulp, and was now staring at him without blinking. "In the end, they overwhelmed us, together with men in white armour on horses between heaven and earth."

"What are you saying, boy?!" he grimaced. "Are you serious?"

Nearby, a slave called Abu Rafi overheard the conversation while fixing up a tent with Lubaba, the wife of the Prophet's uncle Abbas. He'd kept his Islam a secret but was unable to control himself in that moment. "By Allah, those were the angels!" he cried, jumping to his feet. "I knew it! *I knew it!*" He froze, realizing a little too late that people had noticed him shouting something in a triumphant pose. After an awkward pause, he went back to fixing the tent, trying to ignore their irritated looks.

Abu Lahab's face twisted with rage. *"Say that again!"*

"I didn't say anything," the slave mumbled.

Abu Lahab lunged forward, taking out his frustration on the startled man. Abu Rafi crumpled beneath his weight. He tried to shield his face, but the chief's anger rained down in a series of blows that left him blurry-eyed. Everyone in the vicinity watched on in alarm, but it was Lubaba who put a stop to her brother-in-law's despicable behaviour. Pulling out a wooden pole from the half-ready tent, she marched over and swung it at his head.

The resounding crack made onlookers gasp. Abu Lahab rolled off the man and groaned in pain as he delicately touched the open wound. Blood trickled down his sweaty brow and into his thick beard.

Lubaba gripped the pole tightly, her eyes shining with exasperated tears. "Shame on you! You pound away at this innocent man yet *you*, you were too afraid to go and face them yourself?"

Abu Lahab glared at her, fully intending to lash out, but left without uttering another word. He was too wounded— in more ways than one.

I'll get her next time... He promised himself, grinding his teeth, not knowing that revenge should've been the least of his worries.

Though Abu Lahab's attack was misdirected, the same fury that he felt raged wildly in the heart of Hind, Abu Sufyan's wife. She had let out a shrill cry when told that her father and brother—Utbah and Walid—were killed before the battle had even begun. She gripped her husband's sleeve for support and swore to get revenge. "There was nothing in this world more beloved to me than my father, you know that, DON'T YOU?"

"Don't worry my darling, they *will* pay if it's the last thing I do," he promised.

"I don't want revenge. I want them to feel pain and agony," she said through gritted teeth, "the kind that crushes the soul."

Many felt the same way. Looking at the state of their once-mighty army, Abu Sufyan couldn't help but feel responsible. After all, everyone had gone to Badr in the first place because of the exaggerated message *he* had sent. As one of the remaining prominent leaders of the Quraysh, he readily took the reins. This was his chance to stand in the spotlight of leadership and right his wrong.

Like all good military leaders, Abu Sufyan believed in a measured response rather than an emotional one. There was no question that some form of retaliation was required. The prestige of Makkah was at stake, and along with it, the city's long-term livelihood. And so, the younger chiefs of Quraysh acted quickly, sending a message to every household, forbidding the people from wailing for the deceased. They didn't want to show any signs of grief or weakness to the neighbouring tribes, and especially not to the Muslims.

Back in Madinah, throngs of believers rushed out to welcome the Muslim army. The sight of Prophet Muhammad entering the city filled them with joy. Cheers resounded in the streets.

"*Allahu Akbar!*"

"Allah's promise was true all along."

"And look, they've even managed to capture some prisoners."

"This is a miracle!"

Such was the magnitude of the news that many of the remaining idol-worshippers in Madinah embraced Islam. It seemed as though everyone was moved by the miraculous victory— that a small group of Muslims had beaten the mighty army of the Quraysh. Even the hypocrites came to greet the returning soldiers. Despite the resentment blazing in their hearts, their absence from the celebrations would have exposed them, so they took the chance to come out and gloat: "This victory is proof of our people's superiority on the battlefield!"

However, the Muslims were convinced the victory had come from Allah and not their own skill. The miracles that unfolded at Badr reinforced the certainty in their hearts that they *were* on the right path. This newfound level of conviction was the true victory.

As family and friends pressed forward to congratulate and embrace their loved ones, many also searched for faces that were no longer around. It saddened them to learn that over a dozen Muslims had been martyred at Badr, including the Prophet's cousin Ubaydah. However, the Prophet had a reassuring message that made them smile through their tears: "The souls of the martyrs now rest in the bellies of green birds that are perched on the trees of Paradise."[18]

The injured soldiers were immediately sent to the medical tent at the Prophet's Mosque. The tent's beige form stretched from one row of palm trees to the next, the sharp scent of herbs and balm wafting from inside. Rufaydah, the daughter of a renowned physician, was in charge of this operation. Upon hearing of her expertise, the Prophet had given her permission to set up in the courtyard where she would treat the community and train the women to become nurses. The area bustled with activity. Volunteers scurried back and forth carrying bowls of steaming water and armfuls of cloth while the soldiers sat waiting their turn on straw mats.

A handsome man stood out from the row of people lining the pathway to the mosque. His eyes gleamed with fresh grief as he joined Prophet Muhammad's side. "Uthman!" the Prophet said, greeting his son-in-law.

Uthman had not participated in the battle since he had to stay behind to care for his sick wife. Before leaving, the Prophet had reassured him, "You will get a reward and a share similar to someone who has taken part in the battle."[19]

And so Uthman had hoped to welcome his return with the good news of his daughter's recovery. Instead, with a heavy heart, he informed the Prophet of Ruqayya's passing. "We had barely dusted our hands after her burial when the news of victory came..." he explained.

The Prophet squeezed Uthman's shoulder, whispering a prayer of comfort, his eyes brimming with tears. He instructed the Companions to escort the prisoners of war to a secure spot, reminding them to treat them well. Then, without delay, he visited his daughter's grave with his family. The lump in his throat grew when his eyes fell on his daughter's resting place. The dirt was still dark and fresh. His heart ached as he recalled their last embrace.

Some shuffling sounds interrupted the quiet moment. A few people had tagged along in support. Sniffling, they couldn't help but express their own heartache. Although her time in Madinah was short, Ruqayya had earned the fondness of the community. She was admired not only for her beauty and character but the fact that she had participated in two migrations for the sake of Allah; her heart was not attached to a particular land, but wherever she could freely worship her Lord.

Ruqayya had once thought that she would lose the Prophet when she migrated to Abyssinia, but it turned out that it was the Prophet who would lose her. With misty eyes, he glanced beside him at his youngest daughter, Fatimah. He gently dabbed her wet cheeks with the corner of his cloak, and then raised his hands and prayed for their beloved Ruqayya. No one left the gravesite with dry eyes.

When the prisoners of war were led away from the main residential area, they wondered what would become of them. Much to their surprise, some of them were taken away to have their wounds checked. They now sat in quiet anticipation, feeling wary despite the good treatment they had received on the way to Madinah. A few men directed fiery glares at the Muhajirun guards they recognized.

"Traitors," one of them said under his breath, only to be elbowed by his comrade, who gave him a warning look. "What? Whatever they have in mind for us can't be good…"

Abul Aas, the Prophet's son-in-law, was sitting beside the pair and had been quietly inspecting the rope that bound his hands. "They have treated us kindly so far, even though we tried to kill them," he reminded them, the truth of his words silencing any objection.

"Perhaps this is one of the teachings of their new religion?" one of the captives said in amazement. The rest remained suspicious, observing the Muslims with hardened gazes as they awaited the humiliation that typically occurred in warfare.

However, instead of heavy-handed taunts, they were handed wheat bread. After all, the Prophet had ordered the Companions to treat the captives in the best manner, which they readily obeyed. Though some of the captives refused the food out of pride, the others tucked in appreciatively. It did not escape their attention that the Companions were offering them bread while they made do with dry dates whilst on duty.

Among the captives were fierce opponents of Islam and those who answered the call of war out of tribal loyalty; the Prophet's cousins and his uncle Abbas were among this lot. Abul Aas watched curiously as Abbas was led away, disappearing behind a curtain. The two armed guards repositioned themselves in front of the entrance. Abul Aas dropped his gaze, wondering if his father-in-law was still the same soft-hearted man, now that he was in a position of power.

Abbas stood face to face with his nephew. Although Prophet Muhammad maintained the professionalism of a leader, there was a familiar warmth in his expression that his uncle was glad to see.

The Prophet was relieved that Abbas had survived the battle. It bothered him to see his uncle's hands tied up. This was the man who had supported him during the persecution in Makkah, and again during the Pledge of Aqabah. The Prophet was also aware that he hadn't opposed his wife, Lubaba, when she accepted Islam. However, the Prophet had to be fair; it would not be just to set his uncle free without consequences just because he was family.

"Ransom yourself, your nephews, and your friend," he told his uncle. "You are a rich man, after all."

Abbas shook his head, refusing to pay. "The people made me march with them, not knowing I am a Muslim!" he explained.

The Prophet considered this. "Allah knows best what is inside your heart," he said. "If what you say is true, then He will surely reward you. However, outwardly you fought against us." He held his uncle's gaze, his tone softening. "Try to pay the ransom."

Abbas argued that he had no money. His eyes widened in astonishment when the Prophet asked about the gold he had left with Lubaba. "By God! No one knew of that except my wife." Then a peaceful feeling washed over his heart. "Truly, you *are* the Messenger of Allah!"

The Prophet was both happy and relieved to hear his uncle's verbal acceptance of Islam. They promptly arranged for the ransom to be paid so that he could return to Makkah. For now, Abbas would keep his Islam secret and alert his nephew of any dangers.

One exception *was* made for the prisoners of war. It was a strategic decision for the benefit of the Muslim community. Those who were literate could earn their freedom back by teaching ten children how to read and write. Ever since the first Revelation of the Qur'an—"Read!"—Muslims were eager to learn, none more so than the children. They preferred learning in the shade with their wood tablets and reed pens instead of playing in nearby gardens. In this way, Madinah's literacy levels would increase, significantly improving their trade prospects and future negotiations. When the children became proficient at reading and writing, the Makkan prisoners were free to leave. However, many became Muslim and chose to stay in Madinah to live with the Companions.

It wasn't long before the people of Makkah sent money for the captives' release. The Prophet's eldest daughter Zaynab had remained in Makkah with her husband, Abul Aas, who loved her dearly. He treated her well but had refused to become Muslim and ended up joining the Quraysh army. Now that he was a prisoner of war, his parents resented Zaynab more than ever. Their remarks pained her, more so when they insulted the Prophet. Everyone made sure she knew: "This is all because of *your* father."

The looks of disgust from neighbours every time Zaynab went out made the situation almost unbearable. Keeping strong, she fetched a small box from her room and gave one last loving look at the item inside. Everyone expected the worst of her father, but she would show them otherwise. Abul Aas would be returned unharmed. Zaynab was sure of it. And so, she sent her most prized possession to Madinah—the necklace her mother had given her as a wedding gift. When it landed in the Prophet's hands, his tears flowed.

The Companions were taken aback as they watched Prophet Muhammad cry. Nearly moved to tears himself, one of the men broke the silence. "O Messenger of Allah, what is it about that necklace that moves you this way?"

"This belonged to my beloved wife Khadijah," he explained, and they understood his reaction at once. His first wife held a space in his heart that was irreplaceable; he would often reminisce with anyone who knew her. "Seeing this reminds me of my days with her," he said.

"Was it sent by Zaynab for the ransom of her husband Abul Aas?"

The Prophet nodded. He felt for his daughter. Life in Makkah must not have been easy for her, with the Quraysh still enraged by their recent defeat. He also knew how meaningful this item was to Zaynab. As he looked at the onyx necklace, the past tugged at his mind, evoking memories of his beloved wife.

The night before Zaynab's wedding, Khadijah had unpacked her precious necklace with great care and excitement. She had smiled fondly, holding the gleaming necklace against the moonlight. The Prophet recalled the scene so vividly. His eyes prickled with unshed tears. He missed her. Seeing the necklace only increased his longing for his daughter. After losing one of his daughters, he could no longer bear being apart.

Turning to face them, the Prophet addressed his Companions, "If you'll permit it, I would like to free the prisoner and return both him and the necklace to his wife in Makkah."

They agreed wholeheartedly, moved that he had even asked.

The Prophet then sent for Abul Aas. He'd always held his son-in-law in high esteem for remaining with Zaynab despite his family's pressure to divorce her. They'd done everything they could to separate the couple when Zaynab embraced Islam. In those thirteen years of prophethood, Abul Aas had never uttered a bad word about Muhammad. His presence at Badr could only have resulted from family pressure.

When Abul Aas entered the room, the Prophet told him he could return to Makkah. "But understand this," he added, "Zaynab is a Muslim and she belongs here with her people. She is from my family, and I want her close to me. So allow my daughter to come to Madinah."

The man paused in thought, considering this with great difficulty, and then he agreed, "I understand." He knew Makkah was not a safe place for Zaynab. They came up with a plan to get her safely to Madinah, and then Abul Aas left early the next morning. He kept his promise, and before long, the Prophet was reunited with his daughter, delighting in her company.

§

Life in Madinah changed tremendously after Badr. The believers went about their day with optimism fuelling their productivity in the farms and markets. Education became even more emphasized by the Prophet, be it the training of nurses, soldiers, or scribes. The Prophet's Mosque served as a community centre, frequented even after prayer times.

The thirst for knowledge was shared by all. Women gathered around Aisha for advice and spiritual guidance. Muslims young and old memorized the Qur'an whenever a new verse was revealed. When Bilal's voice marked the time for prayer, people rushed to stand in the first rows. The change in political landscape was accompanied by a change in prayer direction issued from the Heavens. They now faced the south wall of the mosque; the direction of the Ka'bah instead of Jerusalem.

We see you O Prophet turning your face towards the sky. Now We will make you turn towards a direction of prayer that will please you. So turn your face towards the Sacred Mosque in Makkah—wherever you are, turn your faces towards it.
[Qur'an 2:144]

As a whole, Madinah began to thrive. The victory at Badr boosted its reputation, and previously hesitant tribes now came forward to form an alliance with the Muslims. They became stronger in the eyes of their enemies. Before, certain disbelievers in Madinah would not hesitate to openly dismiss the 'outsiders' or the new faith that swept through their households. Now they decided to play it safe, waiting with bated breath for the revenge attack the Quraysh were sure to launch.

Meanwhile, the Quraysh grappled to maintain their reputation as they became the talk of Arabia. The desire to re-establish their might grew with each passing day. However, Abu Sufyan preferred a calculated approach instead of immediately rallying an army.

Bouncing a small bag of gold in his hands, he thought about the prisoners of war. The Quraysh chief had allowed families to ransom the captives as long as it was done discreetly—the last thing they wanted was to appear desperate! Upon learning of his own son's capture, he had refused to pay for his freedom. "I will not lose twice," he had said, his voice shaking with anger. "Let them keep him for as long as they wish!" As a leading figure, he simply couldn't be seen as accepting defeat.

As the captives trickled back into the city, Abu Sufyan put eyes and ears on them to extract any useful information. Hearing that some of them had become Muslim, choosing to remain in Madinah, felt like a slap in the face. One thing was clear: they needed to put the Muslims in their place.

The leaders of Quraysh were not the only ones craving revenge. Sitting near the Ka'bah in the afternoon shade, two men named Safwan and Umayr bitterly recalled the events of Badr. They spent the entire afternoon lamenting the loss of their great leaders. Their blood boiled as they spoke of Prophet Muhammad and his religion.

"I swear, if I did not have any debt or family to care for, I would go there right now and assassinate Muhammad myself!" said Umayr. He'd been one of the most ruthless opponents of the Muslims for many years, and had proudly spied on them at Badr to get a sense of their numbers. Now that his son was a prisoner of war, he feared they'd treat him with the same harshness he had shown them. His helplessness added to his misery.

"Then do it!" Safwan urged, taking advantage of his cousin's reckless mood. "I will take care of your debt *and* your children. I'll treat them like my own. So...what do you say?"

Umayr's eyes lit up at the suggestion. Without a second thought, he thrust his hand forward for Safwan to shake. "In the name of Laat and Uzza, I will gladly sacrifice myself!"

"If only your forefathers could see you now," Safwan gripped his hand tightly, "they'd be proud!"

The pair then discussed their assassination plot in hushed tones. "For this to work, we need to keep it between the two of us," said Umayr.

Safwan placed his hand on his heart. "I swear not to tell a single soul."

With that, Umayr sharpened his sword and coated the blade in poison before journeying to Madinah. When he reached the outskirts, he secured his camel and roughly wrapped his turban over his face. On his way to the mosque, he passed by a crowd listening to Umar teaching them passages from the Qur'an. He tried sneaking past but made the mistake of darting a weary glance in their direction. Curiosity had got the better of him. Umar noticed the stranger and locked eyes with him.

Umayr felt a chill run down his back when Umar's eyes lit up in recognition.

"That's Umayr!" He shouted. "That enemy of Allah can only be here to commit evil!"

The next moment, his own sword was pressed up against his neck as Umar led him to the Prophet. *The slightest graze and I'll be coughing out my lungs!* Umayr panicked. When the Prophet saw them, he told Umar to release Umayr. Umar stepped back, keeping his eyes trained on the cunning man.

"Good day," Umayr greeted the Prophet.

Watching him carefully, the Prophet answered, "God has honoured us with a better greeting now, Umayr. *Assalamu alaykum* is the greeting of peace— the greeting of the people of Paradise."

Umayr gave a nervous smile. His fingers twitched. He was less than an arm's length away from his target. Through the corner of his eye, he scanned the room and wondered how soon Muhammad's Companions could reach him if he took his chance right there and then.

"Why did you come here?" the Prophet asked calmly.

"I came to ransom my son."

"Then how do you explain the sword?" Umar interjected, prodding his back with it.

Umayr blinked. "Good question!" he said, fumbling for an excuse. "Since…since when have swords done us any good?" He cleared his throat. "But I am here for my son."

"Tell me the truth." The Prophet's tone was patient, but his eyes narrowed as Umayr stuck to his story. "You are lying," he said. "You came here intending to kill me after your meeting with Safwan by the Ka'bah."

Umayr felt the blood drain out of his face as the Prophet repeated their conversation word for word. "How could you know this?" he cried, certain they had been alone when they conspired— he had looked over his shoulders many times to make sure of it! His eyes searched the Prophet's for answers.

"The Angel Jibril informed me," the Prophet explained.

Umayr felt his mouth become very dry.

"And Allah will *not* allow your plan to succeed."

He was stunned. "We called you a liar and rejected whatever good you had brought…" he remarked, "but my conversation with Safwan was not known to anyone else but the One in the Heavens. Praise be to Allah for guiding me to Islam today!" His voice became shaky as his emotions soared. Umar stepped closer and placed his hand on his shoulder supportively. "I… I testify that there is no god but Allah, and that Muhammad— *Muhammad the son of Abdullah*, is the messenger of God!"

The Companions were so caught up in the moment, that they did not immediately notice the Prophet beckoning them over. "Teach your brother his religion and the Qur'an," he told them. And much to Umayr's surprise, the Prophet went further. "And release his son."

Umayr felt a jolt of happiness enter his heart. He didn't expect this kind of treatment. Right then and there, he committed to learning the religion he'd so violently opposed and resolved to return to Makkah to call others to it.[20]

Back in Makkah, Safwan could hardly contain his excitement. "Some good news is coming soon!" he would tell his friends, but as the weeks went by, he grew agitated. He started asking travellers about Umayr and couldn't believe what he heard. "Umayr, a Muslim? IMPOSSIBLE!"

Finally, Umayr returned and Safwan went to see him. When he confirmed the rumour, Safwan stormed away. "I swear, I will have nothing to do with you ever again!"

Although his cousin's words hurt him, Umayr was not discouraged. He had work to do. That same conviction that carried him across the desert on a reckless mission was now directed towards a more noble cause.

The Battle of Badr was a turning point in the Prophet's ﷺ mission during the early days of Islam and was a victory in more ways than one. For instance, Operation Badr has become a landmark example in Islamic history and the Muslim Ummah of the power of divine intervention in times of hardship. It demonstrates that all success comes from Allah alone. After winning the battle, Allah reminded the believers that it was only through His will that they were victorious

It was not you believers who killed them, but it was Allah Who did so. Nor was it you O Prophet who threw a handful of sand at the disbelievers, but it was Allah Who did so, rendering the believers a great favour. Surely Allah is All-Hearing, All-Knowing.

[Qur'an 8:17]

Chapter 7
The Father of Flames

The biggest house in Makkah, once a place of extravagance and parties, stood in silence, except for the groaning that echoed into the alleyway beside it. A putrid odour wafting from the window added to the wretched mood. The agonizing sounds came from none other than Abu Lahab.

The Prophet's hostile uncle had fallen gravely ill ever since Lubaba had smacked him across the head with the pole. He had hobbled off that day thinking he would soon teach them a lesson, but by the evening, a high fever had set in, draining him of all that anger and bitterness. His throbbing wound became septic within a day. The piece of exposed skull oozed with the most foul-smelling substance.

The Quraysh were terrified of anything resembling the plague, and so the corridor next to his room became an area to be avoided. Poking his walking stick out of the curtains of his four-poster bed, he would knock on the stone floor, over and over, calling for help, but none of his family members would respond. Even his wife, who strongly supported him in his enmity towards the Prophet, now wanted nothing to do with him. In this humiliating state, he realized neither his wealth nor his family could help him.

Fifteen years ago, Abu Lahab had dismissed the verses of the Qur'an calling out his rejection and disbelief. Now, as he spent his days cooped up all alone in his room, the words Muhammad had recited played repeatedly in his mind.

May the hands of Abu Lahab perish, and he himself perish!

Neither his wealth nor worldly gains will benefit him.

He will burn in a flaming Fire, and so will his wife, the carrier of thorny firewood, around her neck will be a rope of palm-fibre

[Qur'an:111]

A week after his injury, the so-called 'father of flames', who had tried his best to undermine his nephew at every opportunity, met his death. No one dared to approach his corpse. The smell was too much to bear. After three nights, the stench worsened so much that a neighbour came out to complain.

"Shame on you all for leaving your father to rot!" the man said, wagging his finger at Abu Lahab's sons. He had spotted them leaving for the marketplace.

The three men shifted uncomfortably before blurting out, "But we're afraid we'll catch his disease!"

The old man's hairy face scrunched up in a disapproving look. "The *least* you could do is bury him so the rest of us can—" He paused, cut off by a gagging noise coming from Abu Lahab's youngest son. The other two glanced behind them at the house and cringed. Noticing their reluctance, the neighbour heaved a sigh.

"Come on, I'll help you. Let's get this over with."

As soon as they entered Abu Lahab's room, a thick stench overwhelmed their senses. Hacking and coughing, they ran out of the room and sent for the help of their servants. Abu Lahab's bulky body was eventually rolled onto a length of cloth.

"How do we wash the body?" one of his sons mumbled through his hand, failing miserably to block out the smell.

"We don't…" was the answer.

Attempting to wash the body would have been torturous, so instead, they flung a few pails of water over it. Then they dragged the body over the gritty paths and thorny shrubs all the way to the outskirts of Makkah.

The men got to work, hoping to finish before the red-tinged sky darkened. After arguing over how to lower his body into the grave, they decided to nudge it in from a distance using poles. From a lofty home built on the tortured backs of his slaves, Abu Lahab's resting place was now confined to a hastily dug-up hole in a deathly quiet area. They quickly covered it with handfuls of dirt and stones thrown from a distance. Not wanting to be around the grave any longer than necessary, Abu Lahab's sons hurried home as the setting sun marked the end of the ordeal.

§

Meanwhile, life in the city of Madinah was flourishing. On the surface, things couldn't have been better. The Ansar and Muhajirun tended to their farms and businesses while the youth focused on lessons in writing and learning the Qur'an.

After the Battle of Badr, people from all over the Arabian Peninsula flocked to Madinah, allowing the message of Islam to reach new tribes. New converts left Makkah, seeking refuge within the larger Muslim community. Since many of these people had nowhere to live and no source of income, the Prophet entrusted their care to various households. Everyone did their best to support their fellow believers, which often left the newcomers stunned at the outpouring of kindness.

"*Subhan Allah*! You are very generous," a young couple remarked, accepting a set of clean garments, "we really do appreciate all the help."

Their host family smiled. "We believers need to look out for each other, we are one *Ummah* now."

"Please, you must allow us to return the kindness. Once I find work, I *will* repay you," the husband eagerly offered, but would soon learn that things operated differently here. The hope for rewards in the Afterlife motivated people's actions more than worldly interests.

In time, the number of newcomers increased so much that the Muslim community was unable to take them in. The Prophet invited them to take shelter at the back of the mosque, where a stretch of roof made of palm leaves and branches shaded the area. Bedding and basic items were laid out, and a stone bench was placed beneath the shelter. The group of Muslims living there became known as Ahlus Suffah, the people of the bench.

They spent their nights in prayer and most of the day learning the religion. Some were offered jobs by those visiting the mosque, and those who couldn't find employment got to witness all of the Prophet's classes and sermons. This paved the way for them to become great scholars and experts in the religion. One particular student would soon become known as a specialist in Prophetic sayings: Abu Hurayrah.

Prophet Muhammad felt a deep sense of responsibility for the growing number of people living in the shelter. Since his home was attached to the masjid, he considered them his neighbours. Whenever he received a gift, he'd have a portion distributed to them. The Prophet would also often sit with them or invite them for meals. "The food of one is enough for two, the food of two is enough for four, and the food of four is enough for eight,"[21] he would say. His household, in particular, lived by these words as they led the way in caring for the Ahlus Suffah.

The Prophet's Mosque served as a gathering place, whether for prayers, lessons, or the distribution of charity. From the early morning to the dark of night, it was rarely unoccupied. Even cats lurked nearby, treading around the back where the Ahlus Suffah would offer them what little they had.

One sunny afternoon, a dog strolled by a group of men sitting in the roofless area of the mosque. They were so engrossed in their discussion of a verse in the Qur'an that they didn't notice until it passed by again. One man turned to shoo it away, but the dog jumped on him, drawing back its lips to reveal a big, toothy grin. It seemed to smile with its entire body, panting and happily wagging its tail, as if welcomed there. The man leaned back, shooting an anxious look at his friends, who had jumped to their feet

"What do I do?"

"I don't know… Should we chase it out?"

Just as one of them assumed an intimidating stance, a calm voice chimed in.

"Don't worry."

A tall man from the Ahlus Suffah said, walking casually towards them. It was Abu Hurayrah. Dressed in a patched-up robe and tatty sandals, he had been quietly reciting in the shade, while crushing date seeds that he planned to sell as animal feed. "The Prophet doesn't forbid them from passing through. If they make a mess, he instructed us to pour water over that spot."[22]

The dog backed down, much to the first man's relief. Turning its attention to the one who spoke, it slicked back its ears and tilted its head, letting out a bark as if agreeing. The men chuckled as they sat down.

"Move along, little dog." The taller man gently ushered it to the exit. It barked once more before scurrying off.

"*MashaAllah*! Even the animals feel at home here in the mosque!" they said in wonder, smiling to themselves as they resumed their reflections on the Qur'an.

§

The busy sounds of thudding wood and clattering pots drifted into the mosque. The Prophet's youngest daughter, Fatimah, was hard at work helping to prepare enough food to share with the Ahlus Suffah. The kitchen area was modest but cosy. A few utensils hung on the wall. A small rack of spices and herbs, hand mills, and a clay pot were spread out for grain sorting on a wooden counter. A cooking fire would soon be lit in the small yard, enclosed by a fence of dried palm leaves for privacy. Attached to this fence was a curtain leading directly into the mosque.

Although they didn't always have sacks of grains or baskets overflowing with ingredients, there was always enough food to share. Gratitude warmed Fatimah's heart as she contemplated this. She briefly stepped out into the yard to dust off a cloth and overheard a group of men leaving the mosque. It was nearly dinner time, so she guessed they were invited elsewhere; though many households were unable to accommodate newcomers, their doors were always wide open to share meals.

As she stepped back in, some hearty chuckling from the direction of the shelter caught her attention. With the Prophet's home joined to the mosque on one side, it was easy to look into the spacious prayer area through the small inside window. Some younger Companions were attempting to hang fresh dates on the beams above the shelter and had almost lost their balance. A few men shook their heads while the rest couldn't hide their amusement as the child moaned at his older brother for hoisting him up too quickly.

Fatimah smiled softly. The scene reminded her of her childhood days. Life had not always been easy, especially witnessing the persecution of her family, so she was grateful for every moment she could spend with them. Though she was only nearing eighteen,[23] she felt that she had lived a lifetime. With her mind on her family, Fatimah returned to her duties, not knowing that a new chapter in her life would soon begin.

§

For Prophet Muhammad, one of the joys of returning home was the greeting he'd receive from his youngest daughter. While most would think that a sip of cool water after a long day was rewarding, the mere sight of Fatimah would be a coolness to his eyes. She had grown into a beautiful young lady. A kind and sincere soul, she always did more than expected of her, even as a young child. The Prophet could still recall the day Fatimah had rushed out to the Ka'bah and tearfully wiped off the guts the Quraysh had dumped on his back while he was prostrating during prayer— one of the many times she had gone above and beyond.

As he rolled out his prayer mat made of palm fibre, he thought about his daughter's future. Abu Bakr and Umar had both asked for her hand in marriage. Even though they were upstanding men, the Prophet had politely declined— he already had someone else in mind. Someone more suited to her age.[24] It had been many weeks since Badr, and he felt the time was finally right, so he brought up the idea when he saw Ali the next day.

The twenty-two-year-old froze when the Prophet brought up the discussion, a slight blush dusting his handsome face. The Prophet's affection for his youngest daughter was no secret. Ali was too overwhelmed to respond. Sensing this, the Prophet graciously smiled and changed the topic.

As for Ali, it wasn't as though the idea had not already crossed his mind. In fact, an elderly servant lady had recently suggested Fatimah to him, encouraging him to propose.

"Did you know the Messenger of Allah has already received proposals for Fatimah? What is stopping you from making yours?"

Ali had given a faint smile. "Do I even have enough to get married with?"

"What about your late father? I'm sure Abu Talib must've left something behind?"

"He spent the last part of his fortune protecting us during the years of boycott in Makkah." Despite Ali's explanation, she'd remained enthusiastic and urged him to approach the Prophet.

"If you ask, he will accept. I'm certain of it."

Ali had not expected that the Prophet himself would suggest the same. The thought that he knew of his financial situation, yet still considered him worthy, moved the young man. Before long, Ali plucked up the courage and set out to visit the Prophet for a very important meeting. A formal proposal.

When Ali sat before Prophet Muhammad, it felt different from other times. His older cousin suddenly seemed more imposing, watching him with a curious gaze. But much of the tense atmosphere was down to Ali's own nerves. Asking the Messenger of Allah for his most beloved daughter's hand in marriage would make anyone nervous!

Sensing that he needed a nudge, the Prophet asked, "What brought you here, dear cousin?"

The moment of truth had arrived. Ali could barely speak, out of awe and respect for Prophet Muhammad. Though usually exceptionally eloquent, he struggled to get to the point. The

Prophet understood where he was heading. He smiled almost knowingly as he asked, "Are you here to ask for Fatimah's hand?"

"Yes," Ali managed, nodding. His confirmation delighted the Prophet.

"What good news, indeed!"

After exchanging a hug, the next topic the Prophet asked about was what Ali had in mind as a dowry.

"I'm afraid I don't really have anything to get married with," the young man said truthfully, thinking of his belongings.

"What happened to the shield I gave you?" the Prophet asked, reminding him of its worth. Ali perked up. "I still have it," he said with renewed optimism.

Before things could proceed any further, the Prophet went to see Fatimah. A warm smile graced her face as she stood up to greet him. He kissed her forehead,[25] saying, "My daughter, come, let's sit and talk."

She took a seat, wondering about the unusual twinkle in her father's eyes. She felt he was about to share something big but didn't expect what she heard next.

"It's Ali. He's asking for your hand in marriage."

Fatimah's eyes held a faraway look as she stared down into her lap.

"What do you say?" the Prophet asked. Fatimah held her face to cover the blush on her cheeks. Though he conveyed the proposal in a calm and gentle manner, her shyness overwhelmed her. Such delicate conversations would usually take place between mother and daughter, but since Khadijah had passed away, the Prophet had had to fill that space in his children's lives.

Patting her head, the Prophet told her what Ali had to offer her. "Do you have any objections?"

Too shy to speak, she raised her head and slowly met her father's gaze. He instantly knew that she approved. Smiling brightly, the Prophet said, "Then we must have a wedding feast!"

Ali was elated that his proposal was accepted. He immediately went to the marketplace to sell his shield. With a portion of the money, Bilal assisted in buying perfume for the wedding, and before long, preparations were soon in full swing. Although they all preferred simplicity, publicly announcing the marriage with a feast was an important part of the wedding.

The community was overjoyed when they got the news— the union was sure to be a blessed one! For the next few days, it was the topic of many excited conversations.

"Have you heard? Ali and Fatimah are getting married!"

"I've always thought they were the perfect match!"

Everyone wanted to contribute to the joyous occasion in some way. Grains, figs, and dates were brought. The Companions made arrangements for a ram to be sacrificed and secured some measures of barley. The preparation of the food and bridal room was entrusted to Aisha and Umm Salamah.

Ali's house was a short walk away from the Prophet's. It was small but neat and simply furnished. The women prepared the bridal room, which they sectioned off with a thick curtain. With the help of Umm Ayman, they collected sand from the oasis to soften the floor. She was the servant who had been with the Prophet when his mother had passed away. Working together, the women beautified the space. They prepared a bed of sheepskin, decorating it with a special striped cloth from Yemen.

Aisha went home to fetch the wedding gifts when she heard light laughter ringing through the passage. She passed by one of the rooms and saw the Prophet chatting with Fatimah. They were both smiling. It suddenly struck her how similar they looked. Even as Fatimah got up to fetch something, her brisk yet light walk, with her body slightly leaning forward, resembled her father's. "She walks just like the Messenger of Allah," she said smiling to herself, as she carried on with her task. Later, she joined the other women to finish the final job of perfuming the Prophet's wedding gifts to Fatimah. It was a simple but beautiful assortment, consisting of a velvet dress, a waterskin, and a pillow stuffed with ostrich feathers.[26]

On the wedding day, Prophet Muhammad performed the marriage sermon, declaring Ali and Fatimah husband and wife. They made for a handsome couple in their wedding attire. Ali was of medium height with a stout build, his strong physique contrasting with his quiet, thoughtful expression. His thick beard glistened with freshly applied oil. Fatimah's dark eyes and radiant face shone the brightest that day.

Prophet Muhammad couldn't have been happier for the two; they held a special place in his heart as he had practically raised them both. He missed Khadijah greatly on that day, and so did Fatimah. The wedding feast, though simple, was considered the best in Madinah. Bunches of dates neatly rested between the fruit bowls dotting the carpets that were laid out in the mosque. Everyone enjoyed the meat and barley dish, paired with a drink of creamy milk or fresh water. Celebrations came to an end as the evening approached. With big smiles and cheerful congratulations, the guests left to get ready for Isha, the night prayer.

After prayer, the Prophet approached his daughter's new home. He had told Ali to wait for him there. "Is my brother home?" he asked.

"How can Ali be your brother when he is your uncle's son?" Umm Ayman remarked as she welcomed him in.

"He is my brother, *in faith*," the Prophet said, smiling. He then asked for a pail of water. As he watched the older Abyssinian woman fetch it, he felt a swell of appreciation for her. She had been a motherly figure to him as a child and remained a blessing to his family, now serving as a comforting presence to his daughter on her big day.

Ali greeted his father-in-law enthusiastically as he walked in. Fatimah followed suit, almost tripping over her dress out of shyness. "Be calm," the Prophet softly assured her, "I have given you in marriage to the dearest member of my household." He smiled fondly at the newlyweds standing side by side. Placing his hand in the pail, the Prophet sprinkled some water on them while offering a prayer, "O Allah, bless them and bestow blessings upon them and their children."

The couple went on to live a fulfilling but trying life together. Despite being from the family of the Prophet, they were not offered a life of luxury that would normally be the case for royalty. Nor did they desire that. They gracefully endured any difficulties, working hard to carry out their duties.

Ali worked as a labourer, which involved long hours and hard work. He would often come home with his chest and hands throbbing. Meanwhile, Fatimah would tend to the cattle and grind flour to the point of exhaustion. Although life before marriage was certainly not without sacrifice, she had always had someone to rely on, whether the valuable support of her sister Umm Kulthum, or Umm Ayman and the rest of the regulars in the Prophet's household. Now Fatimah tackled daily life without having anyone on hand to share the load. However, she strove to remain patient and always did her best.

One day, when Ali returned home exhausted from a gruelling day of work, he saw something that made him stop to consider.

His wife was leaning against the wall to catch her breath. She appeared utterly exhausted. He walked over to her, taking her hands in his. She smiled faintly but was surprised to find him frowning. However, it was a look of worry directed at her hands, raw and rough from the hard work. She had been working the stone mill for hours on end to make flour.

Ali gently held her hands to his chest. "I heard there are still prisoners of war under the Prophet's control. Perhaps we can ask your father for a servant to help?" he suggested, but Fatimah was hesitant about the idea.

Eventually, she went to see the Prophet. As always, her father received her with a welcome so warm it eased her. Still, she couldn't bring herself to say what she had come for. "I…I came to check on you and make sure everything is well," she said. When she returned home, she told Ali, "I was too embarrassed to ask!"

The next time, they went together, lending each other courage. As it happened, the Prophet could not spare a servant. "The Ahlus Suffah are my priority, and we do not have enough to feed them adequately," he explained, his expression soft. "I will use the money people pay for prisoners to fulfil that need." The Prophet's eyes shone with empathy for what the two were enduring of financial difficulty.

Although disappointed, they understood. As they left through the mosque, they noticed many more newcomers looking for a spot beneath the shelter. Those already taking shelter there shuffled about and huddled closer together to make space. That night, as the young couple readied themselves for bed, they heard Prophet Muhammad's voice outside. Fatimah hurried to let him in, worried he'd get cold.

"Both of you needn't get up," he said as he entered the room. He sat between them, placing his hands on their shoulders. "My dear Fatimah, my dear Ali," he started. "Should I tell you something better than what you asked me for?"

They didn't hesitate to say yes.

"These words I'm about to share were taught to me by the Angel Jibril," he said. "Say: *Subhan Allah* (Glory be to Allah), *Alhamdulillah* (Praise be to Allah), and *Allahu Akbar* (Allah is most Great), thirty-three times each before bed."

The couple's eyes glimmered in awe. From then on, they treasured these words and never failed to say them. They felt its blessings in their daily life and found patience easier to muster; their hopeful hearts and quiet contentment sustained them. A few months after their marriage, a distant relative of the Prophet offered his home as a gift. He had heard of the Prophet's longing for Fatimah to live closer to him and was all too happy to facilitate this. The Prophet gratefully accepted this gesture. His dearest daughter and beloved son-in-law rejoiced when they learned they could now live as his neighbours.

When Fatimah and Ali arrived at the door of their new home, they could hear the melodious recitation of the Ahlus Suffah, and recognized the blessing for what it was. They gazed at one another, saying "*Alhamdulillah!*" and, holding hands, stepped into their new home.

Chapter 8
Blindsided

An urgent piece of news bolted across the desert in the form of a frantic rider. It had been a few days after the anniversary of Badr, and the Muslims were still overjoyed by the birth of Prophet Muhammad's grandson, Hasan. The new parents: Ali and Fatimah, as well as everyone else in the city, went about their daily lives as normal, unaware that danger was fast approaching...

People browsing the stalls of Sook al-Manakha quickly moved out of the way when a fast-moving horse zipped towards them. The horseman stopped when he recognised a group of Muhajirun and jumped off. "Take me to Prophet Muhammad!" he said, hurriedly. "I come from Makkah bearing important news." He was carrying a top-secret message from none other than the Prophet's uncle, Abbas. After his conversion, Abbas had returned to Makkah keeping his Islam a secret while quietly monitoring the activities of the Quraysh— especially Abu Sufyan.

The Companion Ubay, known for being the best Qur'an reciter in Madinah, told the man to get back on his horse and rode with him to a mosque in the little village of Quba outside Madinah. The Prophet had made a habit to visit it every week, either riding or walking. When they arrived at the village, Ubay walked swiftly past the well and into the mosque.

The man followed closely behind, wiping his forehead. Beads of sweat dripped down the side of his face in a mixture of exhaustion and nerves. He almost walked right into the back of Ubay who had stopped suddenly. Looking over the Companion's shoulder, he saw Prophet Muhammad standing still with his gaze fixed on the ground, his lips moving slowly as he recited verses from the Qur'an. It was a picture of calmness and serenity—just what he needed to calm his nerves.

While waiting in the prayer hall for the Prophet to finish, the man reached under his turban and pulled out a tiny wound-up scroll. He handed it over to Ubay. The Prophet ended his prayer with some words of praise and thanks to Allah. Then he turned to greet the pair.

"*Assalamu alaykum wa rahmatu Allahi wa barakatuhu,* come and sit down".

The travel-weary man was happy to oblige. Ubay unravelled the scroll and began studying the message. "It's from your uncle Abbas," he said, and offered to read it. The Prophet gave a nod, placing his hands on his lap as he listened intently.

"Dearest nephew. As I write this, know that 3,000 men are marching to Madinah, of which 700 are fully armoured. The cavalry is made up of 200 horses, with as many camels as there are men. They've already set out, and are determined to be there within a week!"

The Prophet beckoned Ubay forward to check something on the letter. Sure enough, it had the burnt orange seal his uncle had told him to look out for. The Prophet knew a day like this would come. Others were convinced that the monumental victory of Badr was enough to discourage the Quraysh from future conflict, but now it was clear that they wanted nothing more than to wipe out the Muslims. They had simply been biding their time, nursing a grudge against the Prophet and his followers that they were finally ready to unleash.

"Permit me to add something, O Prophet of Allah," the man requested, his eyes full of concern. The Prophet nodded. The man readied himself to speak, moistening his dry lips before continuing, "I can confirm everything your uncle says. I myself saw the Quraysh send out several envoys to gather the support of powerful tribes. They were summoning them to an almighty war, using gifts and crafty poetry to rile them up. Anyway, what I'm trying to say is," he swallowed hard. "Time is *not* on your side."

"May Allah reward you, my brother," said Ubay. "And how long was your journey?"

"I-I came as fast as I could. I made it here in three days."

The Prophet was touched by the light ache in the man's voice. He narrowed his eyes in thought. The news, however, was certainly troubling. The Quraysh had mobilized their army so quickly and quietly, giving his people only a small window of time to prepare themselves. Even if they had found out earlier, there was no way they had enough men to match the 3,000 heading their way.

Prophet Muhammad felt the pressure mounting as he trotted on his horse back across the volcanic plains separating Quba from the city. The rhythmic hoofbeats pounding on stone did nothing to interrupt his thoughts. He considered the best way to convey the news to his Companions and the few options they could explore. Date palms and dunes sped by as he rode to the city, his mind replaying the last part of the warning: *"They've already set out and are determined to be there within a week!"*

§

As a strategist, Abu Sufyan was like a cunning fox waiting patiently before striking. Unlike his predecessor Abu Jahl, he kept his emotions in check. His plan had been brewing in the background all along, and he had systematically bought the help of nearly all the neighbouring tribes. At last, the time had come for the Quraysh to strike back and redeem their reputation.

As commander-in-chief, he appointed only the best of the best to lead their contingents. One such leading figure was Ikrimah, the son of Abu Jahl. The death of his father had increased his anger and hatred towards Prophet Muhammad. When the mantle of leadership of the Makhzum Tribe fell on him, Ikrimah stepped into the role with his mind on one thing only: revenge.

The memories of Badr made most people hesitant about going to war with the Muslims again, but with so many powerful figures on their side, the Quraysh felt they were on the cusp of victory. When the army departed from Makkah, they had filled the streets, hoisting their polished shields and sharpened swords, much to the delight of the cheering crowd. Anyone who still felt wary immediately became confident upon seeing Khalid ibn Walid among their ranks.

At the front of the army rode Abu Sufyan. His cool, calculating eyes were a stark contrast to his wife's burning glare. Hind sat inside a well-decorated carriage, swaying with every step the camel took. Her expression remained blank, but her mind whirled with thoughts of revenge. It had been twelve months since her father, Utbah, had been killed by Hamza at Badr. Twelve *long* months; and every day had hardened her, tightening the cog in her gut, winding up her anger, her fury. A turbulent swell of anticipation rose in her chest when she saw the outline of Mount Uhud in the distance.

Hind couldn't help but grin when she heard that the rich businessman Jubayr had offered his Abyssinian slave Wahshi the prize of freedom if he assassinated Hamza. He too, was in search of revenge, as his uncle had also fallen at the hands of Hamza. Tall, dark, and exceptionally skilled, Wahshi was known for his prowess with a spear. Never had he missed a mark. For this reason, Hind made sure to encourage him whenever she spotted him. "Strike with no mercy! Avenge our fallen and you will be rewarded beyond your wildest dreams!"

As they passed the village of Abwa, she suggested vandalizing the grave of the Prophet's mother. But even the most venomous of the Quraysh thought that would be going too far. Hind shrugged and stared straight ahead, remaining silent for the rest of the journey. The other women may have been there to cheer on their husbands and sing songs, but she was there to witness *and relish* the enemy's downfall with her own eyes. Only something as grotesque as digging up a grave could get close to satisfying her rage.

Eager to restore their might, the army of the Quraysh travelled at high speed with their sights set on revenge.

§

Madinah was on high alert. Almost a week had passed since the urgent letter had arrived, and Prophet Muhammad had organized frequent rotations to keep watch for the approaching army. Scouts branched out, instructed to report back on any sign of suspicious activity.

Mus'ab, the first ambassador of Islam to Madinah, was on his way back from patrolling an area that should've been evacuated by now. The people living on the outskirts had been instructed to set up temporary shelter within the city centre, where they would be safer. As he passed through a narrow valley, he tugged his horse's reins to slow down and avoid colliding with a wandering sheep. The animal let out an annoyed bleat before rejoining its flock.

An elderly shepherd smiled apologetically and ushered the animals ahead while his family followed suit, carrying all their belongings in their arms. Mus'ab offered to take some of the load. "Allow me to help you, uncle."

"Many thanks! May Allah reward you." The shepherd said, dipping his head in gratitude. "It's not easy having to shift one's belongings so suddenly…but you people have more important matters to attend to now."

As one of the earliest Muhajirun, Mus'ab was well-acquainted with sacrifice. He insisted on helping, and reached out to accept one of their bundles from his wife. "I'll have someone deliver this to you later today, *insha Allah.*"

"May Allah grant you victory against His enemies," she said.

Mus'ab continued on with his duties. From the vantage point of his horse, he watched some of the last families from the area making their way past the signature palm trees that marked the threshold of the oasis city. The time was now midday and the heat was beginning to bite. As he secured his horse beneath the cool shade of a tree for a short rest, a well-built man on horseback trotted over to meet him.

"*As-salaamu alaykum*, brother," greeted Hamza, as he dismounted.

"*Wa Alaykum as-Salam*," Mus'ab replied, smiling. "Well, if it isn't the Lion of Allah!"

Hamza gave Mus'ab a hearty hug and then leaned back, saying, "You never called me that in Makkah. Did you?" He unwrapped the tail of his turban from around his grinning face,

revealing his strong nose, full beard, and a trimmed moustache
that wrapped neatly around his lips.

"Don't be *too* courageous in this battle, okay?" Mus'ab said,
still gripping Hamza's hand. "You know how much your nephew
loves you."

"Any news from the other patrols?" Hamza enquired.

Mus'ab rolled his eyes at the lack of reaction to his remark. "Not yet. We've sent our best scouts further ahead, but so far there's been no sight of the enemy or any suspicious activity outside of Madinah."

The two began walking. "What about the *other* issue?"

"I looked into that matter. All I can say is that Ibn Ubay is definitely up to something. Since the news arrived, he's been meeting up with a group of his closest associates every night. They have guards on watch while they hold secret talks inside. A few nights ago, some outsiders were spotted coming from the direction of Uhud to meet with him."

Hamza raised an eyebrow causing a frown to appear on his broad forehead.

"Why doesn't the Prophet just shun him?" Mus'ab asked, with an edge of irritation in his voice.

"Allah knows best. Keeping him close may be the best strategy," Hamza reassured him. "I know my nephew. He's not one to be fooled." Then, with an appreciative nod, he excused himself and slung his signature bow and arrow across his back. It was his turn to oversee the training of their newer recruits, most of whom were still awestruck ever since they had learned that he'd hunted lions for sport. Suffice to say, the people of Madinah were relieved to have such a renowned warrior on their side.

The next day, the scouts confirmed the enemy forces had reached the valley beneath Uhud. Although the Quraysh did not seem to be making preparations for battle just yet, they had cleverly setup camp in between Madinah and the rocky mountain range of Uhud, thus preventing the Muslim from having the protection of the mountain behind their back during battle.

Abu Sufyan looked out at Madinah from his tent. A general's banner flapped above; a gust of wind revealing the outline of the idol Hubal painted in the middle. Draped in a luxurious but practical cream robe, he stood out against the backdrop of the dark war tent, his arms folded behind his back. The tribal chief was not interested in invading the oasis city; this was all about redeeming the status of the Quraysh and settling the score with Muhammad and his followers.

Ibn Ubay had been keeping him well-informed of the divisions in Madinah. Abu Sufyan therefore knew there were disgruntled groups, like some of the Jewish tribes and polytheists, who did not approve of Muhammad's authority, and he intended to capitalize on it. He sent a calculated letter to the leaders of Aws and Khazraj: "Be at peace, O people of Yathrib. We share a history together that goes back decades. This new affair that has taken place, you do not need to get involved with it. This is a matter of Quraysh versus Quraysh. Let me deal with it. Send Muhammad with the rest of our people to me."

Panning his eyes over the huge Quraysh army, he felt confident he had blindsided the Muslims. Before retiring to his tent, he informed his soldiers to allow the thousands of animals they'd brought along to recklessly graze on the barley fields of Madinah. It was time for them to make their presence felt.

With trouble now on their doorsteps, Prophet Muhammad called for a council of war immediately after *Zuhr* salah, the noon prayer. All the doors to the mosque were closed. Only the seniors of Madinah and ranked soldiers were told to remain. The mood in the usually peaceful prayer hall became sombre as the Companions waited for the Prophet to begin the meeting.

The feeling of being trapped is experienced by all of us at some point in life. Sometimes it can seem as though the whole world is coming together to harm you. There are enemies you're aware of, and others who conspire from the shadows. It is important not to panic or become paranoid—even if you feel helpless. When the Prophet received the alarming news of an army of 3,000 well-trained soldiers coming to attack, he felt the pressure starting to escalate, but didn't buckle under it. He stayed calm and began to think of ways he could navigate the situation. This is how Allah wants his believing slave to respond in times of crisis. Don't run away from your responsibilities, but don't be hasty and act without consideration either. Islam is the middle way.

Chapter 9
Treachery

The Companions faced the newly built minbar; a simple wooden block on which the Prophet stood to deliver his sermons. They listened carefully. The weight of the situation began to climb as the Prophet explained.

"I propose we fight from within. Our men would be stationed at every entrance into the city while the women and the young would attack from rooftops."[27]

Although the Prophet was inclined to this idea, he valued the opinions of his Companions, and so he invited them to share their thoughts.

Ibn Ubay was the first to speak up. "We have never left this city to attack an enemy without suffering heavy losses, and none have entered this city without suffering losses. So yes, let them come." His words earned a scattering of nods, much to his delight. "I guarantee they will struggle and return home having gained nothing but disappointment and frustration."

His confidently delivered argument made sense, and many senior Companions voiced their agreement. The believers would have the advantage with their intimate knowledge of every alley and cul-de-sac, every vantage point and hiding place. However, the only reason Ibn Ubay was quick to back this plan was because the last place he wanted to be was on the battlefield! In fact, he'd already decided beforehand with his fellow hypocrites to support the view of fighting from within the city.

"So, it's agreed then!" Ibn Ubay announced, a smug smile lingering around the corners of his mouth.[28]

The Prophet noticed that some were not so keen on this idea, particularly the youth. The lack of enthusiasm in their eyes spoke for itself. He signalled to one of them to speak his mind. A young man from the Ansar straightened up and turned a little to face the crowd.

"The Quraysh want a war, *right*? Well, let's give them one!" he said boldly.

"The thing is," another young man chimed in, scratching his head, "we weren't able to fight at Badr and witness the kind of miracles that some of *you* did." He gestured towards a group of the Muhajirun.

Ibn Ubay's eyebrow twitched. He sensed where this was going. It made him uncomfortable. The tide was slowly shifting in favour of this *other* position. He stood up to speak but was too late. A third man, again someone who hadn't participated in the Battle of Badr, had shot up on his knees, ready to speak.

"Exactly. Last time, Allah the Almighty sent three thousand angels, *yes*?! This time," his voice rising in excitement, "MAYBE HE WILL SEND FIVE THOUSAND!"

A roar of "*insha Allah!*" erupted in the mosque. Ibn Ubay tried to interrupt but his voice was drowned out as everyone began speaking over each other in excitement. It was clear that many of the Muslims who were absent at Badr wanted to be out there fighting, punishing the Quraysh for all the troubles they had caused.

"SILENCE!" Ibn Ubay said sternly, finally managing to cut in as the crowd's noise began to taper off. His voice was commanding enough to quieten down the remaining murmurs of approval. As a leading figure in the city's politics, he was used to being listened to. He quickly softened his tone and continued, "Why don't we let the noble Messenger of Allah speak? *He* is our master, leader, and guide, after all."

Ibn Ubay had been keeping an eye on the Prophet the whole time, noticing that he had not yet shown any sign of enthusiasm towards this new idea. If he could just get the Prophet to restate his original view—which was in line with his own—it would sort everything out the way he wanted. He lowered his head with a slight bow towards the Prophet, hoping he would take his lead.

Just then, an elderly man from the Aws Tribe stood up. He cleared his throat, and with teary eyes began to speak of his son who had not survived the Battle of Badr. "Last night, I saw him in a dream. My son."

For God's sake, will you people not be quiet? Ibn Ubay lamented to himself.

"He looked so handsome and was enjoying the fruits and rivers in the Garden of Paradise…" The man blinked away his tears, and placing a wearied hand over his heart, he continued. "He invited me to join him there, for Allah's promise is true! …I am old and don't wish to die in my bed. Lead us out, in the name of Allah, straight to the battlefield where martyrdom awaits us!" he pleaded, looking directly at the Prophet.

This emotional scene tipped even more people in favour of this second view, including Hamza. The Prophet made a heartfelt prayer for the old man before issuing the final verdict.

"Then we will go with *this* plan. And march out tomorrow, *insha Allah.*"[29]

When the sun reached its peak the next day, everyone gathered for Jumuah. The Prophet's sermon that Friday emphasized the importance of sincerity and being steadfast when fighting in the way of Allah. He quoted a verse from the Qur'an that seemed like it was revealed just for this occasion.

"O believers! When you face an enemy, stand firm and remember Allah often so you may triumph."
[Qur'an 8:45]

Eager to hang onto more of his blessed words and advice, many remained near the mosque until it was time for the next prayer. After *Asr*, they finalized their preparations and streamed into the streets, heading home to bid farewell to their families. It was time to suit up for war.

Prophet Muhammad appointed his blind but trusted Companion, Ibn Umm Maktum to stand as leader in his absence. He then met with Abu Bakr and Umar, who accompanied him to his home to help him get ready. The Prophet wore not one but two coats of mail as armour. It meant carrying a heavier load, but he knew full well the Quraysh would make him the number one target of their attacks and needed to take the right level of precaution. The garments made of linked metal rings fitted snuggly over his broad shoulders.

Abu Bakr wound a turban around the Prophet's helmet while Umar inspected his sword for faults, confidently handing it over once he'd finished. The Prophet strapped it in the leather belt on his armour. He then slung a thick wooden shield over his back and together they stepped out of the house.

Waiting outside was a group of young men. They stared in awe at the Prophet's attire.

"What brings you here?" he asked them.

The young men sheepishly looked at their feet until one of them spoke up.

"O Messenger of Allah, earlier at the meeting you were gracious enough to ask us for our view *even though* you had your own. *Subhan Allah!*" His voice began to trail off creating an awkward silence. "We made a mistake. That's what I'm trying to say. Who...who are *we* to offer our view? In fact, we feel as though we've imposed our view on you," he said, as the others started nodding along. The young man continued, "Now that we've reflected, we think *your* initial plan was far better. So please let us go back to that."

The Prophet looked at the row of regretful men before him. "It is not fit for a Prophet to remove his armour once he has donned it,"[30] he said, his usually soft tone now replaced with the firmness of an army commander. "So, in the Name of God, go forward with the decision that was made. Victory is yours *if* you remain steadfast!"

Though reassured, they hesitated to leave because of what the Prophet had *not* said. He hadn't disagreed that his plan was better.

"Indecision has no place in warfare," Umar explained in an elderly-brother manner. The wisdom of the Prophet's words began to sink in, and their motivation rose. The group of young men headed off, hoping to be the first to reach the rendezvous spot and lead the march out of the city.

While the Muslim soldiers were bidding their loved ones goodbye, the hypocrites huddled together to conspire with Ibn Ubay. Behind closed doors, they could be their true selves. Pouring drinks from shiny pitchers, they sat in a spacious room lavishly decorated with patterned rugs and curtains of silk.

"What are we supposed to do now?" A recent recruit leaned forward, his fingers digging into the fancy cushion beneath him. "This is *not* the plan you told us about."

"Ah," Ibn Ubay's eyelids drooped over his eyes, veiled and secretive. "But it is…"

"Oh! You mean we won't have to head out with the rest of them? Great!"

"No! We still need to march out with them," he said, cutting the man's celebration short.

Some of the men cocked back their heads in confusion. "We're not going to fight…and yet we *still* need to march out?"

Just then, a laugh loud enough to rattle the cups bellowed from a hefty, thick-limbed man leaning against the wall at the back. They turned, staring at the nearly seven-foot-tall man whose dark brown hair fell over his tanned face as he bent over in laughter. Julas was Ibn Ubay's sidekick, a Jewish man who had told everyone he'd become Muslim but was only interested in the huge sum of gold Ibn Ubay had promised him. In turn, Ibn Ubay would use his Jewish connections to facilitate communication between him and the Quraysh.

"This is *too* easy! It really is," Julas continued laughing in a deep-bellied way. "And Muhammad is making it even easier by listening to his crazy followers." He straightened, wiping the corner of his eye. "Have you seen how he bends to the views of his followers? I mean, what kind of leader does that?!"

The others joined in the laughter, shaking their heads in agreement. Even those who weren't aware of the plan, like the new recruit, joined in as though they were. They trusted Ibn Ubay and were willing to follow him blindly.

Ibn Ubay leaned back in his chair, watching them with satisfaction. He was proud he still had a semblance of power. *Soon*, he thought, *I'll be the leader of this city just as I was supposed to—before this imposter showed up.*

"Enough now! Go and ready yourselves for battle," Ibn Ubay instructed the group. He smirked. "And make sure our men are seen at the front, leading the march."

Later that afternoon, the Muslim army set out for Uhud, a handful of riding animals trotted between the groups of men. Only a hundred of the one thousand soldiers wore armour; a sword and coat of mail were expensive items that only a few Muslims could afford. Many were hoping to get their hands on the armour of the Quraysh as part of their war-booty for winning.

Also marching out with the men were a group of brave women. They stuck together, carrying supplies and wearing earnest expressions, unafraid of what lay ahead. The Prophet's nearest and dearest, Aisha, Fatimah, and Umm Ayman, leaned in, discussing the inventory of supplies. Walking a few paces behind them was Rufaydah, the medical expert who'd successfully treated the wounded from Badr. She was briefing a large group of volunteers. Their mission was to set up makeshift hospitals near the battlefield so they could swiftly tend to casualties.

The Prophet's aunt, Safiyyah, led a smaller group of women carrying waterskins. She surveyed the troops as they marched passed her until she caught the glance of a tall figure walking by. She gave the soldier a sharp nod and a warm smile. It was her son, Zubair. They didn't need to exchange any words; the gesture was enough to convey her support. Zubair tightened his grip around his sword and dipped his head in respect. His mother's stern but loving guidance had helped shape him to be the fierce warrior that he was. She was counting on him to defend the Prophet and their religion.

Front and centre of them all was Prophet Muhammad, leading the way to the mountains in the north. With a bow over his shoulder and a spear in hand, he made for a striking image, that of a fearless commander on horseback. The sun slowly arched across the sky. By the time they reached Shaykhayn, the sky was bathed in orange hues, seemingly spilling onto the desert. Two shadowed hillocks indicated that they were halfway between Madinah and Uhud. Here, the Muslims stopped to rest and recharge.

They put down their gear just as Bilal's voice filled the air with the melodious call to prayer. After performing *Maghrib*, the sunset prayer together, the Prophet inspected his troops. While waiting for them to organize themselves, he summoned Ibn Jubair for an important matter.

This young man, being an expert bowman known for his bravery, had been appointed as the squadron leader of the archers. His forearms were beefy and would bulge whenever he shook hands with someone—the telltale sign of a well-trained archer. Slinging his bow further back over his shoulder, he quickly jogged over to receive his orders.

"I need your men to keep to their positions over on that hill." The Prophet pointed westward towards a distant rocky hill, an ideal vantage point for the archers.

"Don't leave your positions, even if you see..." he trailed off.

Eight boys, far too young to participate in the battle, had caught his attention. They were craning their necks and standing on their toes, thinking it would help them appear taller for the inspection. It didn't. The Prophet instructed them to go home. They started pleading with some of the elders to intervene. A man from the Ansar came to vouch for one of them.

"This boy, Rafi, is fifteen years old but is the best archer of his clan," he assured the Prophet. As if on cue, the boy jumped into position. His pointy elbow shot back as he drew his bow, aiming at a tree some fifty metres away. The arrow hit the trunk dead in the centre. Impressed, the Prophet allowed him to stay.

An orphan boy named Samurah puffed up his chest, saying, "But I can beat Rafi in wrestling any day!"

The Prophet gave them a chance to demonstrate. The two teenagers stood opposite each other, circling slowly until both pounced forward. Samurah swung around the back of Rafi and tripped him over, ending up mounted on top of him. Rafi waggled his legs, trying to break free. Samurah beamed proudly. He had proven himself to be talented enough to join. The pair waved goodbye to their friends who weren't as fortunate, trying but failing to hide their excited grins.

The Prophet patted their heads before shifting his focus back to Ibn Jubair. Taking him by the arm, he said, "Even if you see vultures devouring our corpses, do not leave your positions. Not until I order you. And likewise, if you see the enemy fleeing the battlefield. *Don't. Leave.*"

By stationing the fifty archers on the hilltop, they could unleash their arrows and thwart any cavalry attack from one of the two remaining open flanks, making it even harder for the Quraysh to overwhelm the Muslims with their superior numbers. It was an excellent strategy— so long as they followed it.

"We hear and we obey," said Ibn Jubair.

The Prophet then moved ahead of the group and started surveying the surroundings. The next task was to figure out how to get to that hill without the Quraysh spotting them. He considered this, well aware that the enemy hoped to lure them out into the open, where they would be outnumbered with nowhere to hide. He was determined, however, to make up for the uneven numbers with a careful strategy.

Prophet Muhammad summoned the clan of Harithah to advise on how to proceed. They were known for having the most expert guides who knew the land like the back of their hands. Grateful that the Prophet extended his trust to them, the guides said, "Don't worry, O Prophet. We will lead you to a position that will stun the enemy!"

Taking advantage of the remaining daylight, the march continued, now under their instruction. It was a much longer route to Uhud and involved moving through narrow valleys and across fields belonging to farmers.

When night fell, campfires sprung up. A few soldiers spread their mats next to the foot of a mountain and sat down to relax. They gathered around the fire, where a slaughtered goat was being cooked, and invited others to join them. Fat sizzled on the fire. The smell of roast meat was almost enough to drive their worries away.

The crunch of footsteps on sand made Rafi spin around; in times of war, everybody was on tenterhooks. But it was just Abu Bakr who had come to give some of the younger soldiers company. For many of them, this was their first battle with the Prophet. And for some, like Rafi and Samurah, their first taste of war.

Ali opened a small sack of dates to share and handed out strips of dried fish, which they singed in the dying embers of the fire. The men shuffled about to make extra space as more joined and then settled down with tired sighs and groans of contentment. Soon the goat was ready. A soldier began tearing off pieces of meat using thick palm leaves and passed them around. They sucked every shred of meat and fat off the bones and crunched up every morsel of crisp, salty skin.

"Isn't it pleasant to think that Paradise will be like this?" Abu Bakr's soft voice floated over the crackling sound of campfires. "Rivers that are more beautiful than anything we can imagine. Even more beautiful than the Euphrates...if you can imagine that."

The young men looked at Abu Bakr thoughtfully as he spoke.

"I heard someone say that in Paradise, there is a tree so big, one can walk in its shadow for a hundred years without covering the distance...or something like that," said Samurah.

This seemed too spectacular to be true, and so the men turned as one to Abu Bakr, as if to receive confirmation. "Actually..." Abu Bakr paused, adding to the already building anticipation, "it's a hundred years *on horseback*."[31] He smiled as they all marvelled at this fact.

"*Subhan Allah*, how magnificent Paradise is!"

"To think, it's better than anything we could ever imagine."

The group continued discussing the wonders of Paradise, wearing smiles as they spoke of the eternal bliss, magnificent palaces, and unimaginable flavours and fragrances that they all looked forward to.

"I can't help but fear for the times ahead of us though," a young man suddenly muttered, earning some wary looks as they were brought back to the present dilemma.

A moment of silence rang out before one of them sighed, "That's how I feel too. I was supposed to get married later this month." He shook his head slightly. "Now I'm not so sure."

A hum of agreement flowed through the group, the mood shifting as their minds drifted to the army that awaited them. "Three thousand men..." an older man muttered, bowing his head to his knees. "Two hundred horses against our fifty..."

"And on top of that, Khalid bin Walid is leading their cavalry!"

"Who?" Rafi blurted. But by the look on everyone's faces, he realized he was probably the only one who didn't know.

"He's as courageous as he is intelligent," one of the Muhajirun explained. "Ferocious in battle and very charismatic.

It's said that one hundred elite soldiers from all over Arabia have joined his battalion. They have their own tailor-made armour and weapons that are imported from Persia. In fact, I think a few soldiers from Persia have joined his battalion."

Rafi stared at the man with raised eyebrows.

"See, that's the other problem we have," said another person. "Our armour is so old and worn out, it barely offers any protection at all. Most of us can't afford the good stuff like those people."

The youth gulped, and the group fell into a thoughtful silence. Hoping to lift their spirits, someone mentioned the glory that was within their grasp. "Can you imagine though," he said "how much war booty we'll get if we win? All the armour and weapons you can possibly carry!"

"*When* we win." Someone corrected him, adding to the sense of optimism. Another chimed in, "straighten up and keep your eyes on the prize!". He said, playfully pushing his companion's shoulder.

Abu Bakr furrowed his brows. Although probably unintentional, the group's motives were slowly becoming worldly and materialistic. He gently steered the conversation back on the right track. "I was there at Badr. And I truly believe that the *only* reason Allah sent His angels was because our intentions were pure."

"I completely agree," said Ali, sharpening his sword. He was one of the youngest who had attended that battle.

"So, if we fight with sincerity again, Allah *will* facilitate our victory— leave everything else in the Hands of Allah." Abu Bakr stood up, straightening his armour. "Now, enough of this gloomy talk."

Even after he had left, the calm of his demeanour remained with the group and the men found their mood had improved considerably. Although some were still understandably nervous, they returned to their tents, turning their concerns into quiet supplications before retiring to bed.

§

The Muslim army woke up during the last part of the night and continued their march. They lit the way with torches, the flames flickering in the cool, dark air as they moved around the barley fields to the jagged ancient lava flows beside them. This sharp, uneven ground was impassable for the large Makkan cavalry.

The Muslims carried on until they reached the stony grounds of Shaut, a short walk away from Mount Uhud. The air felt tense but everything seemed right on track. With weapons resting on the ground, they performed the dawn prayer. When they prostrated, the touch of the cool sand on their foreheads filled them with peace. As they rose their heads, they felt their minds clear. It was the calm before the storm.

The first signs of daylight crept in as they dispersed. The soft yellow of a new day tinged the horizon, revealing just how close they were to the enemy forces. The guides from the clan of Harithah had managed to lead the army around the enemy camp and sneak up behind them. The Muslim army was now wedged in between Mount Uhud and the large hill the Prophet had previously pointed out to Ibn Jubair. This position used the natural environment to shield them from the two flanks. The move was recognized as a stroke of genius by everyone. However, no sooner had the Muslims set up camp than the hypocrites struck the first blow.

"Wait! What do you think you're doing?" a Companion by the name of Ibn Haram said, running forward. He was a poor man who had eagerly answered the call of battle, entrusting the care of his daughters with his only son. He gripped Ibn Ubay's shoulder, more out of concern than anything else.

However, the chief of the hypocrites didn't take too kindly to it.[32] "Let's go," he said flatly to his men, roughly shrugging his shoulder away.

"Come and fight in the way of Allah," the older Companion urged, "or at least help defend?"

"What?!" Ibn Ubay yelled back, scowling. The scene began to draw the attention of others. They blinked in surprise seeing a large number of men packing their things to turn back.

Ibn Ubay wanted to ignore Ibn Haram but realized how it might look if he didn't bother to explain himself. He shook his head as though the man had completely misunderstood. "Look, my brother," he said, slipping into his practised pious manner. "We only want what Allah and His Messenger want."

The older man could not believe what he was hearing. "You think *this* is what they want?!" he said, shocked. Were these well-armed men really about to leave?

Coming in closer, Ibn Ubay held the man's face and lowered his voice. "You know deep down that the Prophet wanted us to fight from *inside* the city," he said. "So why don't *you* join *us*?"

Ibn Haram glared at him balefully. He leaned in so his face was an inch from Ibn Ubay's. "I will *not*," he said, then pulled back. "In fact, I really doubt *this* is your reason for turning back."

"Well tell me then, which wise person chooses the opinions of boys knowing it could get them killed?"

"*Wallahi*, I will cut out your tongue if you're referring to the Prophet!"

"Calm down, my brother. All I'm saying is that we know better than to expose ourselves out here. We will fight, but *not* from a position of weakness."

Ibn Ubay's words were completely empty, for he never truly intended to participate. He wanted to cause the very bewilderment and confusion he saw rippling through the ranks as more people noticed the commotion.

The older man stepped back, simply saying, "Remember, Allah knows the secrets we keep..."

Ibn Ubay proceeded to abandon the Muslim army. Three hundred soldiers followed him, some who were in on the treacherous plan, like Julas, and others who had been misled. The loss of a third of the Muslim forces at such a crucial point nearly broke the army's morale. It was like a rug had been pulled out from under them.

Hamza and Mus'ab shared a look, both remembering their previous conversation. A sense of foreboding rippled through the camp. "How can seven hundred of us stand a chance against three thousand?" some soldiers said worryingly.

One may wonder why the Prophet didn't decide to revert to the original plan of fighting from within the city, especially when he thought it was better. No one would have refused to listen had he done so.

The Prophet knew that in times of war, a moment of indecisiveness or hesitation could be the difference between life and death. The general must command his army with clear and precise instructions. If he had been swayed by the young men to go back on his decision and change the whole plan once people had started carrying it out, it would've created another, far greater problem: breaking the confidence in the leader. Umar understood that better than anybody else and tried to explain that to the young men when he said, "Indecision has no place in warfare."

Chapter 10
The Fatal Mistake

In the face of what should have been a setback, Prophet Muhammad remained calm and collected. He redirected his army's focus on the matter at hand, urging them to remain steadfast. On his command, the senior Companions began issuing instructions to their troops to get ready for battle.

The Harithah and Salamah clans, from the Aws and Khazraj Tribes, were too dismayed to listen. The departure of the 300 soldiers had them teetering on the brink of withdrawing.

Ibn Haram had noticed their panicked muttering growing louder, and like others witnessing the commotion, he badly wanted to reassure them. He took half a step forward, then stopped. Considering how his advice to Ibn Ubay had fallen on deaf ears just moments earlier, he started hesitating. Before he could finish thinking of the right words, the crowd parted, making way for the Prophet. Ibn Haram sighed with relief and stepped back.

The Prophet walked over at speed; those following him had to take two strides for every one of his. Ibn Haram watched as he spoke at length with the wavering clans—even though he had not done the same to Ibn Ubay and his men. *Is the Prophet aware of something that the rest of us aren't?* He wondered.

He tried desperately to listen in and catch some of the Prophet's wise words, but the loud beats coming from the drums on the side of the Quraysh made it impossible. Instead, he watched in admiration as the men's expressions shifted.

The effect of the Prophet's presence was immediate, and their change of heart was obvious. They stood straighter, taller, with conviction renewed.

The morning's chill slowly started to give way to the heat of the day. White banners flapped in the breeze coursing through the emotionally charged area.

Of those given the privilege of hoisting a war banner was Mus'ab. As the first of the Muhajirun, there was no one better suited to wave their flag. The banner of Aws was hoisted by Usayd, a leading tribesman who had set out to confront Mus'ab for preaching, only to find his heart moved by the Qur'an. The banner of Khazraj was held up by Hubab, a prominent member of the tribe and a respected warrior.

"Know that paradise lies beneath the shadow of swords,"[33] the Prophet told the army, reminding them of the rewards for fighting in the way of Islam. "But I forbid you from harming women and children."[34]

Hamza, leader of the infantry, exchanged a hardy nod with Zubair, now in charge of the modestly sized cavalry. Neither of them lacked any motivation to fight, but the Prophet's speech stirred their emotions and raised their morale even higher. Leaders and followers were now ready to fight with all their might. At the Prophet's command, Ibn Jubair led his fifty archers up the hill to get into position and load their quivers with as many arrows as they could.

"Prevent their cavalry from approaching our brothers from the rear. Guard their backs and don't leave your positions, no matter what," Ibn Jubair sternly reminded the soldiers as they all trekked up.

The Prophet looked at the main body of soldiers lined up in ranks. Raising a sword high up in the air, he asked, "Who will take this sword and give it its right?"

Every soldier desired to be picked for the privilege, and many stepped forward, including Umar.

"Let me take it!" Zubair volunteered enthusiastically, but the Prophet asked his question again, this time adding, "Who will take this sword *and* give it its right?"

A Khazraj swordsman known as Abu Dujanah came forward. "And what is its right?" he asked.

A wise question, Umar thought. They were all eager to see who the Prophet would choose.

"Its right," the Prophet said, "is for you to strike the enemy with it until it bends."

Abu Dujanah squared his shoulders and raised a hand, saying, "O Messenger of Allah, *I* will take it and fulfill its right."

The sword was almost three feet long from tip to hilt. It was double-edged with a two-handed hilt, making it heavy, too heavy for an untrained soldier to use. But Abu Dujanah was no ordinary soldier. To him, it looked perfect. He'd carried heavy swords since his youth, falling in love with combat when he was in his twenties. Grinning, he accepted the sword and started inspecting the blade. It was long and beautifully straight, a handspan wide, with wavelike serrations at the base of the blade.

Zubair stood there observing Abu Dujanah's delight. *Really? Am I not more deserving of this sword than he is?* He wondered. There and then, he decided to keep an eye on him and make sure he lived up to the responsibility the Prophet had given him.

Abu Dujanah tightened his grip around the hilt and felt the sword become part of him. He could sense energy racing along its blade, as if it were eager. He paced forward into the open desert until he was in full view of the enemy lines. He reached into his pocket and pulled out a red bandana, which he proceeded to tie around his head. Then he began to strut around, menacingly waving his sword in the air.

"This is a type of walking Allah does not like...*except* in situations such as this,"[35] the Prophet remarked to the Companions as they watched him. Upon his command, the army rallied down the slopes of Mount Uhud, and Abu Dujanah fell back in line. Despite their suddenly shrunken forces, the Muslim army was ready to fight.

The risen sun warmed both air and earth as the armies faced each other. Each army's front row was now close enough for arrows to reach the other side. It was the Quraysh that dominated the landscape.

3,000 men clad in bold hues of earthen green, burnt orange, and black, covered the plain. Khalid fronted the cavalry of a hundred soldiers atop rare, well-trained horses. His men stood to the right of 1,200 spearmen. Another hundred horsemen flanked the left, led by Abu Jahl's son Ikrimah, his expression as severe as his blade. Behind them were continuous lines of heavy-footed, bright-eyed men in thick armour with large maces and metal shields.

Abu Sufyan stood out in the lead, an olive cape decorating his jet-black armour. From his horse, he reminded the flag bearers of their important role. The banners symbolized the army's glory and were not to fall for even a minute. The men bristled, determined not to fail in their task as they had at Badr. They kept their eyes glued on the Muslim army, whose white and beige garb stood out against the tanned-yellow mountain behind them. The Quraysh would have laughed at their small numbers had they not feared a repeat of the events at Badr.

Mus'ab stood a little ahead of the Prophet and hoisted the Muhajirun's gleaming banner high. He looked at the familiar faces glaring at him, locking eyes with the enemy's main flag bearer.

The army of the Quraysh marched forward as one until the heavy scents of woody incense carried over to the Muslim's side. Those at the very front could feel it catching the back of their throats. The enemy stopped and straightened out their ranks. The Muslims could now see the thick fumes of incense rising out of brass pots being dangled by slaves stationed in between the enemy's troops.

Abu Sufyan came forward and called out, "O men of Aws and Khazraj. I ask again, leave my cousin to me and we will all turn back. We have no reason to fight you. This is the last time I ask. What do you say, my brothers?"

Weapons and voices rose in protest. The Ansar took offense at his pointed disregard of the Prophet's presence. Abu Sufyan's face hardened at their rejection. He cursed, scanning across the groups of Aws and Khazraj. They showed no sign of wavering.

"Your army is half made-up of men too small to fight properly!" he yelled at them. "Almost makes a man think you *want* them to get killed." Then he turned, offering a permissive nod at the sneering man behind him.

Abu Amir approached, loudly introducing himself as a fellow tribesman from Madinah. "You have heard from the leader of the Quraysh, now hear me! I am one of you. A son of the Khazraj Tribe. I am Abu Amir, the Noble One."

"Ha! You stopped being one of us when you left after Badr. Now we call you Abu Amir *the Evil One*," Usayd responded. The pair of them had been close friends and business partners. After embracing Islam, Usayd had tried very hard to convince him to accept the message. Instead, Abu Amir moved to Makkah and allied with the Quraysh after seeing how the Muslims gained the upper hand after Badr.

"You have been bewitched by this man's words. He has caused families to split and insulted our forefathers. He's even—"

"If you want to keep your head attached to your shoulders," Abu Dujanah said, pointing his sword at Abu Amir, "think carefully about what you say next." He took ten paces forward and raised a challenging eyebrow, keeping the sword steadily fixed in the man's direction.

Impressive, Zubair thought as he looked at Abu Dujanah in his poised stance.

"I see I am not the only one who thinks you shouldn't fight," Abu Amir continued, to which some Muslims soldiers exchanged awkward looks. "Do you not see the wisdom in Ibn Ubay's decision? Follow him and be safe."

"Are you finished?" Umar asked.

The simple question left Abu Amir flustered. Some of the Muslims began to laugh, and he quickly realized the old tribal loyalties he was banking on had been uprooted and replaced by something far, far stronger. Their newfound faith had given them extraordinary unity and loyalty towards each other. Abu Amir had clearly overestimated his esteem. He scurried back, his face flushed as he avoided Abu Sufyan's sharp gaze.

Abu Sufyan raised one arm. "Advance!" he ordered, and the army started marching forward. His wife, Hind, led the women on the sidelines, beating drums and rattling tambourines.

The women came to a halt at a spot they deemed safely out of range and began chanting to the flag bearers and soldiers marching ahead. "O sons of Abdud Dar, go onwards. Strike violently with your swords." Now and then, they would cry out,

"Praise Laat!", followed by, "Praise Hubal!", and lastly, "Praise Manaat!". They cheered and chanted to rile up the soldiers, and then, suddenly, there was silence. The drumming and chanting stopped just as Hind's melodious voice soared through the ranks. She sang an old war-song, tugging at the soldiers' pride:

"We are the daughters of stars,
We tread on silken carpets.
Advance and we will embrace you.
Retreat and we will leave and never love you."

In doing so, she made a point that every man understood clearly—it would be the height of cowardice to flee the battlefield in full view of their womenfolk.

The Muslims kept their eyes trained on the opposing army in silence. The enemy seemed to fill the horizon, more of them snaking down the sloping dunes in the distance as the drummers resumed. Young Samurah's eyes widened in horror; he hadn't expected the Quraysh army to be this big. The aggressive beating of drums sounded like a thunderous stampede invading their ears, and making the encounter more intimidating. He glanced around anxiously. Many others looked unsettled too.

Ali gave the boy an encouraging pat on the shoulder as he strode by, making his way to the very front, where the Prophet stood on a slightly raised edge with Abu Bakr and the others. "The plan is working, O Messenger of Allah," he said. "Can you see? As they approach us, their ranks are being squeezed due to the hill."

The Prophet and his senior Companions all noticed Khalid break away from the main body, making his way around the hill to attack from the rear. His men followed closely behind.

"Let him go and meet the arrows of Ibn Jubair," Umar remarked confidently.

Just then, a fearless soldier from the Quraysh raced out on horseback, challenging the Muslims to an opening duel. "I am the ram of the battalion! Who will fight me?" His bravery was such that few were eager to face him.

Zubair accepted the challenge and walked forward. He fell into an aggressive posture, using one of the swordplay stances taught to him by Hamza. The enemy soldier danced backward, blade at the ready. He moved far more nimbly than one would expect for a man in such bulky armour. Zubair swung first but the man skipped to the side making him miss— but only by an inch. Feeling a thrill at the contest, the soldier dashed forward and attacked downward with an over-hand blow, trying to hit Zubair's helmet. Zubair ducked, going down on one knee, letting him to cleave empty air, before leaping back up and thrusting his blade towards the soldier's open chest. The powerful blow was enough to end the contest.

"*Allahu Akbar!*" the Prophet proclaimed. The signal to charge swiftly followed. Umar, Abu Bakr, and Ali followed the Prophet as his horse picked up speed. The army of Quraysh swarmed forward, meeting the charging Muslims. Soon, whinnying horses and battle cries resonated as fierce fighting broke out.

The first major blow came when the Quraysh flag bearer was hit by an arrow. His brother jumped to catch the flag but was struck down as soon as he reached it. Another quickly hoisted it just as Hamza shot forward, valiantly swinging two swords. Hamza and Abu Dujanah split the enemy ranks with their expert swordsmanship. One by one, the family of Quraysh flag bearers fell as the battle raged on.

A loud scream from the rear pierced through the cacophony of battle sounds. Hearing that her two sons had died, the woman swore to get revenge in the most gruesome manner possible, earning an approving look from Hind, whose hatred ran just as deep. "Don't worry, Sulafah," she said. "They don't stand a chance. Our moment will come." She whirled around to face the other women. "Louder!" Hind commanded, refusing to have their chants drowned out by the clanging and crunching of weapons and bone.

A woman who vastly differed from her was Nusaybah of the Khazraj Tribe. Her reason for being on the battlefield was not revenge but love for the Messenger and Islam. Armed with a sword and bow, she had followed her husband and two sons into battle. Nusaybah was also one of the two women who had sworn allegiance during the Second Aqabah Pledge. With her heart spurred on by that precious memory, she shot arrow after arrow at the soldiers who tried approaching the Prophet.

Amid the frantic scenes, the Muslims had each other's backs. They were quick to create a pathway for the injured to return safely to the foot of the mountain, where the nurses were stationed. The women worked quickly to treat wounds and supply weary fighters with water. Graceful as a wave, their medical unit moved forward down the slope as the army gained more ground.

The archers up on the hill made sure a curtain of arrows rained down on anyone who dared to approach, keeping Khalid's cavalry well at bay. Ibn Jubair kept a keen eye, thwarting their attempts thrice. Shoulder to shoulder, the archers worked as a team. Eventually, Khalid ordered his men to back down, choosing instead to move further back and around the mountain until they disappeared from view.

Abu Sufyan steadied his horse and quickly assessed the state of his troops. His men were struggling, and Khalid's cavalry was nowhere to be seen.

How did they organize themselves so well? He kept asking himself. *How? We gave them no time to prepare! It's not possible in seven days to*— He was sharply jerked out of these thoughts when he heard his own name being shouted out.

"Abu Sufyan! My master! The flag bearers...they'll *all* down."

For the first time, the Quraysh leader felt his resolve begin to waver, while the sight of the fallen flag bearers made the Muslim army throw their weight behind their strikes even harder.

"Take that!" Abu Dujanah grunted. His fiery bandana quickly became a sign of havoc as he slew his opponents. He paused to flex his fingers, bouncing his sword in hand. An enemy soldier hurtled forward, thinking he would catch him off guard, but instead fell, crashing to the ground as Abu Dujanah ducked and used the momentum to lift him up and over.

When he wasn't deflecting crushing blows, Zubair kept a look out for the courageous swordsman. Deep down, he was upset that the Prophet hadn't honoured him with the sword and had even thought to himself: *But I am the son of Safiyyah, his aunt.*

Abu Dujanah darted past him, on the hunt for larger, particularly violent opponents. One such man seemed to only target the wounded, so Abu Dujanah went after him. He raised his shield, blocking the sword that greeted him. The enemy yelled, stabbing at him with his spear. Abu Dujanah casually knocked the weapon aside and rammed into the soldier. The man grunted as he toppled over, cursing when he realized the red-turbaned warrior had trapped his sword under his foot, leaving him wide open. Abu Dujanah swiftly brought down his sword.

Zubair watched the encounter unfold in all its glory. It was then he understood the Prophet's decision. *Allah and His Messenger truly know best*, he said, smiling to himself. Abu Dujanah happened to meet his gaze and grinned with satisfaction. Zubair smiled back, but Abu Dujanah's head had already spun away to track down a nearby voice urging the enemy to keep going.

The person was shouting orders in a mad frenzy, throwing fallen weapons to the soldiers. Abu Dujanah leapt forward, lifting his sword ready to swing, when the person stumbled back, shrieking, "NO!"

He paused to take a closer look, a looming silhouette against the stark blue sky. It was none other than Hind. "I respect the Prophet's sword too much to disobey him." Abu Dujanah said through gritted teeth, sword still poised to strike. He had clearly heard the Prophet forbidding the killing of women and children. Hind ran for her life.

Nearby, an enemy named Ibn Qamia frowned as he shook his bloodied sword. He saw men backing away from the red-turbaned warrior but was well-acquainted with Abu Dujanah, having trained with him many years back, long before their friendship had soured. He considered himself a better fighter and was eager to prove it. Motivated by the desire to outshine his friend-turned-enemy, he set off to stalk the Prophet Muhammad in search of glory.

With her heart thumping wildly, Hind ran back toward the other women. On her way, she spotted the familiar slender form and short afro of Wahshi. The Abyssinian appeared to be standing aimlessly, or worse— hiding. She lashed out at him, "You coward! What are you doing *here*?" He blinked at the hysterical woman. "Go, go, you're wasting precious time!" She didn't realize that he had spotted Hamza and was waiting to pounce.

Wahshi brought a finger to his lips. He shifted his eyes to the spear in his hand and then to someone behind her. She looked over her shoulder, grinning wickedly when she saw the blur of a familiar ostrich feather close by. Delighted, she stepped out of the way and to find a safe spot to watch from.

Wahshi had been quietly waiting behind the tree for the chance to strike, his mind and eyes fixed on one man alone. The man who would earn him his freedom. Hoping to go unnoticed, he had ducked behind various bushes and rocks while following his target. Hamza was instantly recognizable. The warrior fought with unmatched prowess wielding *two* swords. The edge of his black turban flapped in the wind as he out-maneuvered his opponents. Wahshi didn't even need to look out for the ostrich feather pinned to his chest to know who he was. Nor did he have to be close enough to hear him declare, "I am Hamza, The Lion of Allah!"

The Abyssinian slave was now far enough to be safe, but close enough to strike. He pulled a long red ribbon from his pocket and attached it to the end of his spear, an ancient custom his father had taught him when he was a child in Africa. As Hamza neared, Wahshi froze, gripping his spear in his sweaty hand. The Prophet's uncle was now dealing with a man trying to scoop up the enemy flag. As he lifted his sword above his head, Wahshi spotted a vulnerability in his armour. He jumped into action. Holding the spear aloft, he balanced the tip towards the target as Hamza delivered several blows to the man. He let out a cry as he hurled it, "FREEDOM!"

Being an expert spearman, Wahshi was never going to miss. The ribbon flapped in the wind as his spear cut through the air just as Hamza finished his opponent. Hamza gasped as it plunged into his back. He looked over his shoulder to see who the perpetrator was. Turning his whole body, as if in slow-motion, he began staggering forward to retaliate.

Wahshi felt a spike of fear and took a step back. So strong was Hamza's will that, to Wahshi's amazement, he even tried yanking out the spear. He shut his eyes, mustering all his strength, but the spear was in too deep. The wound proved fatal, and the Prophet's uncle fell to the rocky ground.

His eyes grew distant as he looked up at the clouds, as if he saw things there that no one else could. Every part of his body became still, but his lips continued to move slowly. *"Laa ilaaha illa Allah, Laa…ilaaha illa…Allah."* His last words: there is no god except Allah. A tiny river of blood escaped from the wound on his back. Sword still gripped in his hand, Hamza's once-sparkling eyes were now closed.

When Prophet Muhammad heard what happened, his eyes flashed and his heart plummeted. *My uncle.* He fought through a blockade of warring bodies until he was close enough to see for himself. The ostrich feather was flickering in the wind, resting on top of a lifeless body. The chaos of battle prevented the Prophet from approaching further.

The death of Hamza was a great loss to the Muslim army. Still, they pushed on, assuming control of the battle.

Abu Sufyan's will finally snapped when he narrowly escaped being stabbed. He jumped back, quickly scanning the valley as he tried to catch his breath. The memory of Badr began playing on his mind more clearly than ever before. Sensing a repeat about to unfold, he grabbed a horse and fled without looking back.

Ali shot his most winning smile to the Prophet. "Abu Sufyan and his men are turning back." Another nearby Companion nearly jumped for joy when he saw the troops were indeed withdrawing. "Your tactics worked, O Messenger of Allah!" he cheered.

The Makkan women could be seen scattering in the distance. The jewellery around their ankles glistened as they lifted their skirts to flee. A screaming Hind offered weapons to the retreating soldiers. "No, you cowards! Stay! Fight! Fight!" But her words fell on deaf ears, and soon enough, she had no choice but to run with them.

The Muslim soldiers on the field took this as a clear sign of victory and began collecting the war booty, picking up fallen swords and abandoned armour. The group of fifty archers peered down from the hill, watching as their comrades began to celebrate while collecting the items. They waved their bows high in triumph and began wondering if they, too, could head down and join in.

"Shouldn't we go down now?" one of them asked. Ibn Jubair shook his head. "No. We must stay here."

Some archers frowned; they could clearly see the Quraysh forces fading further into the distance. They stood there waiting, growing more restless with each passing minute. "Look! We can hardly see them now! We've won, so *what* are we waiting for?"

Ibn Jubair couldn't believe his ears. "Have you forgotten what the Prophet said? He gave us explicit instructions NOT to leave."[36]

The men hesitated, each casting uncertain glances at the others...until one said, "I doubt he meant for us to stay here *forever*. Look! I think they're calling us."

The archers glanced over at the Muslim troops in the distance, some hoisting the collected swords and shields.

"By Allah, we're going to join our brothers and take our share in the war booty," one of them decided, making his way down the hill. Another moved to follow him, explaining apologetically,

"The battle is done and the Quraysh have lost. I'm sure of it. Come."

In the end, only ten men remained stationed. They watched in frustration as the bulk of the group sped down the slope. The Prophet's voice echoed in Ibn Jubair's mind. *Even if you see the vultures pecking at our corpses, do not leave your positions.*

He felt a sense of dread building inside his stomach. *Something bad will happen now. I'm sure of it.*

Chapter 11
An Unbreakable Will

"My brothers, come back! Forget about the war booty!" Ibn Jubair's voice called down the hill. But most of the archers couldn't hear him anymore.

Waiting in the wings for precisely this opportunity was Khalid bin Walid. His fully plated armour flashed like a streak of silver as he emerged from behind the mountain. He raised a fist, signalling to his men to halt behind him. They were as eager to fight as he was. Approaching with caution, he counted the number of archers remaining on the hill. As soon as he confirmed the count was only ten, he turned to his men and beat his sword against his shield twice.

It was time.

Khalid thrust his sword into the air, then kicked his horse into motion. His men bellowed a war cry, falling into formation behind him. They charged across the flat, rocky ground, making a beeline for the remaining archers on the hill.

The ten archers tried their best to fend off the men, but soon all their arrows were depleted, and the horsemen swooped in.[37] They fought bravely to the death. Khalid then used the vantage point of the hill to scan the battlefield and calculate his next move.

"We'll surprise them from the back," he told his most senior comrade, pointing to the rear of the Muslim army. Once again, he raised his sword high, and this time, with a flick of his hand, his horsemen moved in like hunters seeking out lone soldiers— soldiers who were completely unaware of what was happening behind them.

Khalid's men swarmed in like vultures around a corpse. "Blow the horn," he yelled, yanking his spear out of the chest of a fallen soldier. The eerie sound boomed across the battlefield and soon reached the fleeing Quraysh soldiers. Those on horses could see the banners that Khalid's squadron was now waving high. They couldn't believe it. Immediately, they stopped fleeing and turned around to form an attacking position. And then they charged.

The first to join Khalid bin Walid was Ikrimah, with his men tailing him just metres behind. The combined cavalry of both leaders swept through the unsuspecting Muslim ranks like a sandstorm.

The first wave of attack stunned the Muslims. Until now, the rear had been successfully protected by the archers since the beginning of the battle. As the returning enemy soldiers closed in on them, they found themselves being sandwiched between the two forces. Overwhelmed, their morale started crumbling as more war cries echoed throughout the valley, marking the enemy's return. The Muslim ranks became a scene of chaos. Spears hit shields, flesh, and leather; men yelled and screamed, not knowing whether to fight the enemy in front or behind. The tide began to turn.

Khalid shouted for the horn to be blown again, encouraging the remaining forces to speed up their return. When the Muslims heard the hooves of hundreds of horses galloping towards them, they were no longer able to defend their position. Many began to flee in disarray, dropping their spears and shields.

Near the rear, the Prophet continued fighting alongside a small group of fourteen men. His best friend, Abu Bakr, stayed by his side.[38] Seeing the wounded and disoriented state of his followers, the Prophet realized the situation had reached a critical point. Something drastic had to be done. The Prophet slammed his visor up, fresh air washing across his sweaty face, and although it would give away his identity, he cupped his hands around his mouth and, using all the energy he could muster, he called out to the fleeing men from the top of his horse, "O slaves of Allah! Stand firm with me. Stand firm with me."

Ibn Qamia was the first enemy to recognize the voice of the Prophet. He flicked up his visor, revealing his snarling mouth. The pitiless glint in his eyes promised nothing but pain. He bent down, grabbed a large, jagged rock, and began sneakily approaching the Prophet's position.

It was too difficult to get the horse to move out of the way quickly enough; the Prophet could only spin around to save his head from the hurtling rock. There was a soft snap, and suddenly the Prophet and his saddle went tumbling through the air. The horse's quick turn, coupled with the rock's momentum, had caused the saddle girth to break.

Ibn Qamia let out a celebratory roar. So violent was the force with which the Prophet's face was struck that he assumed he couldn't possibly have survived. He chuckled, admiring his own audacity. The correct thing to do next would be to go over and make sure the Prophet was actually dead, but he didn't want to. This was the moment of glory he'd been craving since the beginning of the battle. Finally, he'd outshone Abu Dujanah. "I've killed Muhammad! Did you hear me?!" He glanced again at the motionless form of the Prophet, and then, turning to his comrades engaged in fighting nearby, he yelled, "I SAID I'VE KILLED MUHAMMAD!"

"Muhammad is dead!" The rumour spread through the battlefield like wildfire, and the Quraysh began celebrating.

Umar was locked in a fierce duel when he heard someone shouting it out. He froze. *No. It's not possible.* His mind began spinning. *How could the Prophet be gone?*

The enemy soldier saw a wildness shoot into Umar's eyes and fled the scene.

Panic and disorder swelled on the Muslims' side. Pain welled from deep within their chests. "This is because of us…" A few who abandoned their post grieved, frozen as though the world had stopped, while others ran past them to either fight or flee. Some crept up to find refuge in the mountain; it was easy to escape now that the Quraysh troops started slackening. Many Muslims stood their ground, continuing to fight through the chaos. Those who remained steadfast yelled, "We will die as he died fighting for Islam!"

The battle was over as far as the Quraysh were concerned.

"We did it!" Ibn Qamia cheered. "Go tell Abu Sufyan the good news!"

Laughing, a cluster of soldiers kicked sand toward a fearful youth who ran off. They didn't bother giving chase, choosing instead to revel in their victory. With the Prophet gone, they were confident that this marked the end of the new religion. They started repeating the chants their women had made when the battle had begun. "Praise Laat!" followed by "Praise Hubal!" and then, "Praise Manaat!"

§

Prophet Muhammad was not dead. He regained consciousness and rolled over to sit up on his elbows. The first thing he noticed was the laboured breathing of his fallen horse groaning beside him. Wiping the sand from his eyes, he tried focusing on his surroundings. He could hear men in the distance shouting instructions, but their voices were too muffled to make out what they were saying. The smell of fresh blood and trampled earth hung in the air.

As soon as the fuzziness in his eyes had gone, he staggered to his feet and scanned the battlefield. It seemed as though no one was there. He blinked hard a few times and squinted to look again. Most of the Muslim army had fled or were fleeing. The small group of soldiers protecting him appeared to have been killed. The last time he had been alone like this was in the cave of Thawr during the migration to Madinah, but even then, Abu Bakr had been with him.

The right side of the Prophet's face convulsed with pain. Sweat matted his long beard. A trickle of blood running down his cheek made him reach up. The face guard and visor from his helmet had been smashed open by the rock. Feeling a large wound on his cheek, he moved his fingers downwards, passing them over his mouth. He felt a gash on his lip and rolled his tongue against the roof of his mouth. He could taste blood. The impact of the blow had knocked out a tooth.

"How…how can these people succeed," he said, wiping blood off his chin, "when they hurt their own Prophet like this?" His anger was directed towards the Quraysh; the people who he'd grown up with and lived amongst for fifty years. *How could they be so cruel?* he wondered. What hurt the Prophet more, though, was knowing that the archers had disobeyed his command. *Didn't they pay attention when I said: Even if you see the vultures pecking at our corpses, DON'T LEAVE YOUR POSITIONS.* The pain from his tooth wrenched him back from his thoughts. Just then, he heard a familiar voice nearby.

"You're alive!" The words, muffled by a face guard, became louder as a man entered the Prophet's line of sight. He lifted his visor, revealing a huge smile. "*Alhamdulillah*, you're alive!" It was Ka'b, a famous poet of the Khazraj Tribe who had embraced

Islam during the monumental Second Pledge of Aqabah. He'd spotted the Prophet from a distance and recognized his armour.

"Quiet…" the Prophet mouthed, raising a finger to his lips. But it was too late. The Quraysh had noticed the commotion.

Abu Bakr was there in no time, shield at the ready as the enemy began closing in on them. Their murderous shouts caught the ears of nearby Muslim soldiers. Tears of relief sprung to their eyes when they realized it was only a rumour and the Prophet was actually alive. Those with arrows started firing to push back the advancing soldiers, while the others regrouped to position themselves around the Prophet.

Just moments ago, they were frozen in a state of shock, but as soon as they could see the Prophet moving around, their hearts were awakened. All their concerns about losing their comrades or the battle became trivial. The Prophet was alive. With renewed spirit, they rallied around their beloved leader, making a ring formation as Ibn Qamia and his troops drew closer.

"Take that!" A towering man lurched forward through the circle of men, swinging his sword violently. Nusaybah jumped in front of the Prophet, widening her stance. She raised her shield up high to catch the enemy's blow. The man's sword skimmed off it and angled down towards her other arm, crashing into her shoulder guard.

"Arghh!" She roared. Her voice a mixture of pain and fury.

The sword had become stuck in her armour plates, and the enemy was trying desperately to yank it out. Spotting her chance, she ducked under the soldier's arm and thrust the hilt of her own sword into his ribcage, forcing him to stagger backwards.[39]

Another Companion intervened and swiftly dealt the man a mighty blow. It was Abu Dujanah. Like the others now in the company of the Prophet, he had continued to fight through the onslaught of Khalid bin Walid, as well as through the rumour of the Prophet's death—much to Ibn Qamia's dislike. He had come just in time to join the group of brave Companions led by Ali and Umar, protecting the Prophet as they retreated to safety. They fought as one, fending off attacks as they navigated their way to higher ground. Even as the Prophet fought off oncoming soldiers, he kept encouraging his men, "Whoever defends us now is promised their place in Paradise! In fact, he will be *my* friend in Paradise."[40]

More Muslims joined the resistance. The Quraysh quickly realized that these soldiers were not the sort to give up, nor go down without taking someone with them. They began backing off to consider another strategy. When the Companions realized they had successfully warded off the assailants, they spun to face the Prophet. "Who did this to you?" they asked. But there was no time for an explanation. They had to act quickly before Abu Sufyan and Khalid bin Walid caught up with Ibn Qamia's troops.

The Prophet mounted his horse, slammed down the broken visor, and waved to his men, "O servants of Allah, with me. NOW!" He had to ride the horse bareback as the saddle had broken off during the fall. Digging his heels in and pressing with his knees, he brought the horse to maximum speed while urging all his Companions to head towards the mountain.

Soon the sandy earth made way for rocky ground as they neared the foot of Mount Uhud. As the horse's hooves began thudding louder and harder, the Prophet started to feel his shoulder throbbing savagely. He realized he must have landed on it when falling off the horse earlier. Either that, or it was a blow he'd absorbed during battle. Gritting his teeth, he forced himself to keep moving. They were almost there.

Motioning to his Companions to slow down, the Prophet led them towards the entrance of a small glen he'd spotted. It seemed to offer the easiest ascent to a point of safety where they could overlook the enemy's movement. Here, they dismounted from their horses and waited for those on foot before beginning a steep trek up the mountain.

From their horses, Abu Sufyan and Khalid bin Walid watched the retreating men and debated whether to go after them. Although Khalid bin Walid preferred to completely eradicate the Muslims, Abu Sufyan was satisfied with the damage they had dealt that day. The two, however, did agree that it was worth confirming whether or not the Prophet was still alive. They didn't want to rely on the word of another soldier and had to see for themselves.

As the Muslim army worked their way up the mountain, the air grew sharp and the sun began to disappear below the horizon. It was nearly dusk by the time they found a damp but secure enclosure to settle in. Everyone was exhausted.

The Prophet leaned against a large boulder on the edge of a cliff with one foot pressed against the stone. Using a spear he'd picked up along the way, he leaned onto his left side to relieve some of the pain in his right shoulder. The trek up the mountain had drained him of all energy. He dropped the spear beside him, briefly kneeling to see if that would lessen the pain. The concern to check on his remaining soldiers soon yanked him to his feet.

The Prophet turned around and tried lifting himself on top of the boulder to see out, but couldn't raise his right hand high enough, no matter how hard he tried. A Companion by the name of Talha came to his side and knelt down to help. The Prophet placed a foot on his back and stepped up. Peering over the large rock, he scanned the battlefield to make sure none of his men had been left behind. He could see the bodies of fallen Muslim soldiers but none that were still fighting.

Not wanting his gaze to fall on his uncle's body, he began to monitor the enemy's movements. *What are their intentions now?* He wondered.

The ululations and chants of women could be heard. Abu Sufyan had invited them back onto the battlefield to celebrate. A few had gathered around one particular fallen soldier and were dancing. The Prophet dreaded to think who that was. He shifted his eyes away and looked directly below, past the ridges of the mountain towards the foot from where they had come up. Thankfully, it was clear.

Once he was sure no one had been left behind and no enemies were following them, he told his soldiers to be at ease. He praised his Companion as he climbed down, "If you wish to meet a martyr walking the face of the earth, look no further than Talha, the son of Ubaydullah."

Around him, the Companions sat down to rest and recuperate. They began unbuckling their armour and gasping for breath. The air inside the enclosure was thick with humidity, but the cold stony walls of the mountain helped cool them down. Those with enough energy hurried this way and that to search for a nearby stream or puddle.

Ali was the first to find water and scooped up as much as he could using the inside of his shield. He brought it over and held it out to the Prophet, but the smell of stagnant water sickened him. Although the Prophet could not bring himself to drink it, he used some of it to wash the blood from his face.

With a moment to finally think, the mood of the soldiers quickly changed from relief to regret. Thinking about the number of men that were killed—many of them close friends and family members—caused them to grieve. The heavy losses after the initial victory made the battle more emotionally exhausting than anything else. The Muslim army had gone from triumph to defeat in a matter of minutes. A few soldiers began to cry.

"O Messenger of Allah. What— aren't we going back to take the bodies?"

The Prophet looked up. It was young Samurah. He looked as if he had aged a few years in a day. The vibrant sparkle that shone in his eyes when he had first begged to join them earlier was now gone.

"I think Rafi... Rafi is still out there," he murmured, shifting on his feet. "He...didn't make it."

Just then, a commanding voice boomed over their heads. "Is he still alive?"

The words bounced off the mountain cliffs, which amplified them. Every single head turned towards the boulder the Prophet was resting against. They rushed over and peered over the rocks that were keeping them out of sight.

"It's Abu Sufyan...and two other men," Talha said, his voice barely louder than a whisper. "I can't see their faces from here."

"That's Khalid bin Walid and Ikrimah," Umar said confidently. He was so tall he didn't need to stretch to get a look at them.

"Is he still alive or NOT?!" Abu Sufyan's voice was piercing. Some of the men exchanged nervous glances and looked to the senior Companions to see if any of them would respond.

Umar opened his mouth to speak, but the Prophet spun to face him. "Don't respond," he said calmly.

Another question was shouted out: "What about Abu Bakr?" The echo made it seem as though the question was being repeated, much like during an interrogation. Again, the Prophet gestured to his Companions not to engage. Umar gritted his teeth before letting out a sigh. To him, not responding was like admitting the Prophet and Abu Bakr *had* been killed.

"What about Umar?" came the third question, followed by a short pause. "I suppose they're all dead then. So, we're finally rid of those three!"

This time, Umar could no longer control himself. "You're mistaken, enemy of Allah!" he growled. "The people you mentioned are still alive, and Allah has more disgrace in store for you!"[41]

Abu Bakr looked over at the Prophet and saw him shaking his head with a smile. He began grinning to himself and immediately saw the funny side of it too. He tried placing a hand over his mouth to suppress the laughter, but it was of no use. Some of the Companions heard him chuckle and started laughing too, triggering others to join in. It was a welcome release from the tension everyone was feeling.

Now that they had given away their location, the pressure to stay hidden had vanished. They peered over more freely and saw Abu Sufyan's smile turn into a frown. It was *their* laughter that was now echoing into the valley.

Looking up, Abu Sufyan gave them all a hostile glare. Not ready to back down just yet, he raised his sword triumphantly and began cheering rhythmically, "How high is Hubal! How high is Hubal!"

His men joined in.

"Will you not answer him?" the Prophet asked his Companions.

They cocked their heads back. "What should we say?" they asked, wondering why the Prophet had changed his mind about responding to Abu Sufyan's trash talk.

"Say, *Allah* is the Most High *and* the Most Majestic!"

Abu Sufyan scoffed when he heard their response. "Well, we have Uzzah and you have no *uzzah*!" he shouted back at them. His men snickered, nodding appreciatively at his clever play on the word *uzzah*, which, besides being the name of an idol, also meant honour.

Again, the Prophet instructed Umar to respond, "Say *Allah* is our Divine Supporter, and you have absolutely no divine supporter."

The silence they were met with spoke of the chief's growing irritation. The Muslims smiled in satisfaction at this small but meaningful victory. They may have been wounded and forced to retreat, but they refused to have their will broken.

Wanting to have the last word, Abu Sufyan's voice floated over the cliff with a noticeable edge of frustration. "Victory in war comes in turns. Today was for Badr," he said, reminding them of what happened last year, "so now we're even."

Umar replied, "No, we're not. Our dead are in Paradise and yours… are in Hell!"

Abu Sufyan, taken aback by this, decided that enough was enough. Slowing steering his horse away, he said, "If you come down, you'll find your dead have been mutilated," he paused, half turning as if to look at the corpses, "I neither ordered it nor am I sorry about it."

As evening set in, the Muslims bandaged their wounds, shared water, and appreciated the gift of life. The thought of their fallen weighed heavily on their minds, but they recognized the blessing of martyrdom. The Battle of Uhud may not have swayed in their favour, but it was not without lesson. It was a testament to the resilience of the Prophet and his Companions in the face of such a trial. They were able to wade through the turmoil and live to fight another day. And though they suffered heavy losses, they did not lose heart—an incredibly important lesson for the Muslim community today. No matter how bad the situation may get, they should never lose heart, because those on the Straight Path always win in the end. That is the promise of Allah.

Chapter 12
Not The End

Once the Quraysh had left, the Muslims approached the battlefield. Darkness descended over the vast valley. The cool air hung with sadness and fury. Under the hazy starlight, flames flickered from torches in an attempt to illuminate the shadowy slopes. Carefully, they stepped over the battle debris, navigating the area until they reached the first mass of their fallen soldiers. Many of whom had fallen face-down, taken in the back by spears or arrows from the Quraysh forces.

Prophet Muhammad felt his heart drop when he saw the body of his uncle; this was the spot he had seen those vile women dancing earlier on. "There will never be a moment as sad for me as this," he choked out tearfully when he saw what the Quraysh had done to him.

Abu Bakr and Zubair were standing beside him, offering moral support. They had never seen him this upset before. The Prophet knelt down over the body and passed a hand over his head. Hamza was truly everything to him—a dear uncle, a close friend, and a mentor. In his youth, Hamza had taught him how to string a bow and use a sword. During the days of persecution in Makkah, he had his back, ready to defend him. And the day he had declared himself a Muslim was one of the happiest in the Prophet's life.

The Prophet raised his hands to the sky in prayer as tears streamed down his bloodied cheeks. "May Allah have mercy on you, my dearest uncle," he said, sniffling between his words, "you always raced to do what was good."

Zubair kept his jaw tightly clenched as he stood looking down uncomfortably at his feet. He wanted to stay strong for the Prophet's sake, but could feel his throat closing up. The sound of a familiar voice made the Prophet's eyes snap open. He turned around and spotted his aunt Safiyyah marching over to them.

"I have to see him... I have to see for myself," Safiyyah kept repeating.

The Prophet looked over at Zubair. "Your mother! Stop her." He was concerned that she wouldn't be able to bear the sight of her brother, considering how difficult it was even for him.

Zubair rushed over and stood in her way, "you can't mother. There's no need for you to see," he explained. His mother had no intention of stopping.

"Don't you dare." She pushed past him, making Zubair scamper to catch up.

"My mother," he said, catching her by the arm, "the Messenger of Allah is ordering you to stop!"

Safiyyah paused. Recognizing the concern flickering in his eyes, she said gently but firmly, "My son, listen to me, and listen well. I heard what happened to my brother and I will bear it with patience— by the will of Allah. Now move aside."

Unsure what to do next, Zubair looked over at the Prophet. "Let her approach," he said. His gaze softened as his aunt came over.

Safiyyah's strong expression crumbled at once. The sight of Hamza's mutilated body was too much to bear.

"*Oh...my...brother*," she sobbed. "What have they done to you." She collapsed onto her knees. "*No! no, no*. Not like this..."

The warmth of the Prophet's hand on her shoulder grounded her. Safiyyah clamped her hand to her mouth and closed her eyes, feeling the flurry of emotions whirling inside begin to flatten. She tightened her lips into a thin line, her eyebrows furrowing as she inhaled shakily. She then opened her eyes. "I'm okay," she told the Prophet. He looked her deep in the eyes, and she stared back at her nephew, tears glistening on his blood-stained cheeks. Seeing him being strong made her feel strong.

Safiyyah didn't want to lose control of herself like some of the other women on the battlefield had. The sound of them wailing was now clearly audible to her, before that the voices were just noise. She felt her mind clear and began praying for Hamza, concluding her supplication with words of patience: "To Allah we belong, and to Him do we return." The tears through which she spoke stung her eyes but paled in comparison to the pain of her heartache.[42]

Despite Abu Sufyan's warning, no one was prepared for the appalling sight that greeted them. The whole valley had become a scene of carnage. There were cries of pain, howls of despair as loved ones found their fallen family members. There were silent tears too, quiet reassurances whispered into ears: that Allah will reward with martyrdom. The Muslims sombrely prepared to bury the dead, tears welling up as they dug holes in the sandy ground.

In total, seventy Muslims were slain in the Battle of Uhud. The elderly man who had dreamed about his martyred son got to die on the battlefield as he had wished, as did Ibn Haram, who would always be known for his steadfastness and sincere advice to Ibn Ubay.

Mus'ab had done his utmost to hold up the Muhajirun's flag until he no longer could. Once an elite of Makkah, known for wearing fine clothes and beautiful perfumes, he now barely had enough cloth to shroud his body. When the Muhajirun tried to cover his feet with his robe, his head would become exposed, and when they covered his head, his feet could be seen. In the end, they used leaves to cover his feet.[43]

As they buried him, the Ansar came over to join the funeral. To them, Mus'ab was their first teacher. He had brought the message of the Prophet to Madinah, and through his efforts, they had found the light of Islam. They continued to pray for him even after the burial was complete.

Once the last grave was filled, it was time to head home. Prophet Muhammad praised Allah and prayed for the martyrs. The Muslims then set off, their minds grappling with the day's events as they walked by the same scenery they had passed with full confidence earlier that day. Despite dealing with his own grief, the Prophet made sure to stop on the way and console those who had lost their relatives. More than anything, they were glad to see him alive— their relief at his safety helped them cope with their losses with patience.

§

The first Friday after Uhud, the Muslims closed the marketplace just before the sun reached its highest point in the sky. It was time to prepare for *Jumuah*. Fresh faces in clean robes squeezed into the prayer hall to find a place to sit. Ibn Ubay showed up as per usual, wearing his most laidback expression. According to him, he had nothing to be sorry about. If anything, he felt his position in Madinah must have been strengthened after Uhud.

The events had turned out just as he'd predicted: he had been right all along, and it was the Prophet who had placed them all at risk. It had been foolish to engage the Quraysh army on open ground, and they should be thankful that Abu Sufyan had decided not to press his advantage and fight on into the oasis itself. Now they could see that Muhammad's increasing power in

Madinah worked only to their disadvantage. They could believe all they wanted about him being a Prophet, and thus the spiritual leader, but Madinah would surely be wiser to place political leadership in the capable, prudent hands of Ibn Ubay himself. Or so he thought.

But in this, Ibn Ubay had underestimated one of the Prophet's most striking characteristics: the ability to turn tragedy into a lesson.

Within days of the battle ending, the Prophet had been receiving Revelations from the Angel Jibril. The verses of the Qur'an not only pointed out key lessons for the Muslims to take from the events at Uhud but also condemned those who'd refused to fight, labelling them as hypocrites. The Prophet had been actively teaching these Revelations in the mosque, and his Companions had been circulating them among the community for some days now. Even though specific names were not mentioned in the verses, many more Muslims were beginning to connect the dots.

Blissfully unaware, Ibn Ubay held his head up high as he aimed for the front row of the congregation. It was his habit to give a welcoming speech before the Prophet delivered the Friday sermon— he enjoyed the attention it gave him. Before the Prophet mounted the pulpit, he would loudly announce, "O People, the Prophet of Allah is soon to arrive. Hear and obey him so that Allah may bless you." Nobody had said anything about this routine out of respect for his position and social status in Madinah. But this time, the Muslims would react differently.

Ibn Ubay stood up to speak. He began by praising the Prophet, duly emphasizing his relief and gratitude that his life had been spared. Then he couldn't resist praising his own wisdom in having advised against open battle with the Quraysh army.

"Had our brothers listened to me, they would *not* have been killed," he declared— a statement not exactly calculated to win the hearts and minds of those who were mourning their casualties and still suffering from their wounds.

First, there was silence. Ibn Ubay saw their backs stiffen, and their eyes widening. Now he really was the centre of attention— but not the kind he had hoped for.

Then a furious voice called out, "Sit down! You *abandoned* us."

"He didn't just abandon us!" cried another. "He set us up, then betrayed us!" A cascading hum of agreement resounded around the prayer hall.

"What are you people talking about?" Ibn Ubay pushed back. "Because of me, three hundred men of Madinah are still alive and well."

"We know what your *real* reason was for turning away," said Ibn Masud, who was also sitting in the front row.

The crowd fell silent, wanting to hear what he had to say. The young man from Makkah, who was known as nothing more than a poor farmer back then, had now become one the biggest scholars of Madinah. From all the Companions, he was the most knowledgeable of the Qur'an. Now standing just a few feet away from the flustered chief of the hypocrites, he continued criticising him.

"You were playing a game! Weren't you? And now your time is up. In fact, I'm sure it is you who Allah intended in the new Revelations we have all been hearing." And then, before Ibn Ubay could respond, he composed himself and began reciting them:

So what you suffered on the day the two armies met was by
Allah's Will, so that He might distinguish the true believers and
expose the hypocrites. Who, when it was said to them, ***"Come***
fight in the cause of Allah or at least defend
yourselves," *replied,* ***"If we had known there was***
fighting, we would have definitely gone with
you." *They were closer to disbelief than to belief on that*
day—saying with their mouths what was not in their hearts.
Allah is All-Knowing of what they hide.

[Qur'an 3: 166-167]

As the crowd fell silent and nodded solemnly to Ibn Masud's melodious recitation, Ibn Ubay was wracking his brains to think of how best to defend himself. He didn't bother to sit and learn the Revelations from the Prophet like the other Companions did, and therefore had no idea these verses had been revealed about his antics.

"Now be honest… *if* you can," Ibn Masud continued pressing him. "Isn't this precisely what Ibn Haram—may Allah have mercy on his soul— was saying to you before you got up to leave: *Come fight in the cause of Allah or at least defend yourselves?*" he said, quoting the verse of Qur'an, which clearly matched what Ibn Haram had said.

Everyone glanced over at Ibn Ubay.

"Um…*Subhan Allah!*" he muttered. "The words of Allah… so…so beautiful."

Hesitation. Ibn Masud spotted it and wasn't going to let it go unnoticed.

"Beautiful *and precise*. Wouldn't you say?"

And again, everyone glanced over at Ibn Ubay.

"I'm sure that old man said many things, but he never said anything like that to me."

The congregation gasped, appalled by his lies. To Ibn Ubay's relief, his friend Julas was now standing between him and the angry crowd, gently waving his hands downwards to try and calm the mood. The towering figure, who was usually the most laidback person in the room, felt a ripple of panic pass over his face. He was stunned by the verses calling out the behaviour of Ibn Ubay and all his group— which, he realized, also included him!

"Had that old man listened to me," said Ibn Ubay, peering over the arms of Julas, "He'd be here right now, praying with us." It was the best response he could muster up in the heat of the moment, but it only served to frustrate the Muslims even more.

"*Astaghfirullah!*" Ibn Masud said in disbelief. "This is precisely what the Almighty informed us you would say." And again, he composed himself and began to recite:

They conceal in their hearts what they do not reveal to you. They say, "If we had any say in the matter, none of us would have come to die here." Say, O Prophet, "Even if you were to remain in your homes, those among you who were destined to be killed would have met the same fate." Through this, Allah tests what is within you and purifies what is in your hearts. And Allah knows best what is hidden in the heart.

[Qur'an 3:154]

"You enemy of Allah!" someone shouted from the back. The hundred or so glaring eyes now fixed on Ibn Ubay made him panic. He spluttered wordlessly, as he whirled around to leave, pushing his way through the tightly-packed crowd.

When he reached the door, one of the Ansar stopped him. "Wait, my brother. Wait for the Prophet to come, and ask for forgiveness," he suggested.

Ibn Ubay's nose wrinkled in disgust. "And why would I do that?!"

§

For many days, the streets of Makkah were littered with evidence of a big party. It had become a city full of smiles. The fragrance of woody incense and freshly sacrificed animals hung around the Ka'bah. It was a nauseating mixture of spices and blood, but the people tolerated it. For them, it was the smell of success. The same, however, could not be said about their leader. Since returning to Makkah, Abu Sufyan had been living in his head, unable to shake off a niggling thought.

No doubt they had killed plenty of Muslims, but had they achieved their key objectives? The Quraysh had set out to get rid of the Prophet, secure their trade routes into Syria, and restore their prestige in Arabia. However, it seemed as though only one of these had been achieved, and even that was questionable. When these thoughts became too heavy to carry, he called for a meeting in Darun Nadwah.

Every seat around the table in the torch-lit chamber was occupied by either a chief or a general. Their chattering and laughter bounced off the stony walls. Abu Sufyan took his place at the head of the group.

"May you all have a long life," he said, trying to sound upbeat, though his face looked gloomy and detached. "Khalid bin Walid, Ikrimah, and Ibn Qamia— may Laat and Uzzah honour you for coming. I wanted my generals here along with the chiefs, so I summoned you too."

They raised their wine glasses in appreciation. Once all the servants had left the chamber, Abu Sufyan rose to speak. The men around the table watched him carefully; they could see their chief was uneasy about something.

"I have called you all here to discuss the battle. There's some outstanding issues that must be…well, discussed." Abu Sufyan's voice had now lost its enthusiastic tone.

"Like what? We won. Nothing else to discuss." Amr ibn Aas said, waving a hand. He was the shrewd politician who had tried to persuade Najashi to give up the Muslims who had fled to Abyssinia eight years ago. The Abyssinian king had flatly refused him. The memory still burned in his mind.

"*You* might call that a victory, but I cannot celebrate knowing the women of this city saw us running for our lives," Ikrimah said angrily. "And then there's the issue of my father— may he rest in peace. I cannot…no, I *will* not consider Uhud as proper revenge either." He relaxed his clenched fists as his outburst ended.

So I'm not the only one who thinks it wasn't a victory. Abu Sufyan thought.

"Don't be so hard on yourself. You fought well…when you returned, that is," Amr ibn Aas said with a cheeky grin.

Khalid bin Walid chuckled. "Who knows, if I hadn't sounded that horn, you might have run all the way to Taif!" Ikrimah dipped his head, as if ashamed.

"You can take credit for getting rid of the archers, but no one came as close to killing Muhammad as I did," Ibn Qamia boasted, flashing a toothy grin. He crossed his bulky arms and leaned back, remembering the moment he had cornered his target.

"Yes, and a fine job you did of that. The man is alive and well, still lurking up there in Madinah." Amr ibn Aas said, pointing northwards. "In any case, I consider the battle a victory. We avenged our fallen at Badr and put Muhammad back in his place." The thin moustache that ran all the way around his mouth made his smug smile look comical. A couple of chiefs nodded in agreement.

Abu Sufyan sat there with his hand on his chin, listening to his men as they continued going back and forth over whether they could call it a victory or not. It seemed to go on for ages. He'd thought the meeting would help relieve the tension in his mind but, if anything, it was giving him a headache. He glanced over at the window cut into the clay wall. It was almost night time, and his wife had made him promise he'd be back to entertain some guests.

Hind had become a lot calmer after Hamza's death. Thanks to Wahshi, revenge for her father and brother who had both been killed at Badr, had finally been served. Even so, Abu Sufyan dared not provoke her temper by breaking his promise. He took a deep breath and sighed. It was time to draw the discussion to a close.

"Yes, yes, you all raise fair points, but what was our aim? What did we hope to achieve from all of this…the money that we spent in raising the army, the efforts we made to fight them, and the casualties we suffered as a result?" he said, throwing his hands in the air as he stood up. "What was the point, eh?"

Abu Sufyan took a long pause waiting for someone to answer. No one did. His aggression was making them uncomfortable, but more than that, they wanted to see where he was going with this.

"It was to kill Muhammad once and for all, no?" he pressed on. The men all nodded, murmuring in agreement. It was an obvious point, but they had all missed it. Abu Sufyan voice began climbing in agitation as he continued. "And was it also not to take back everything he's stolen from us: our trade route to Syria, our position in Arabia, and our children who *he* has misled…"

Amr ibn Aas opened his mouth to defend his view, but the chief was not done just yet.

"And there's another problem. Something you've all missed."

The men leaned forward over the table, listening intently.

"It's become clear to me that we have a spy among us."

They all jerked upright at that. "What! What do you mean? Who?"

"Think about it. Someone must have informed Muhammad about our plans to attack."

"But they were poorly prepared…*no*?" Ibn Qamia said, tilting his head quizzically.

"But prepared they were!" Abu Sufyan snapped, slapping the table with the palm of his hand. "They shouldn't have been. How did they even know we were coming? Did you not notice how they managed to position themselves to take advantage of the valley and that hill?"

"That's correct," Khalid ibn Walid said thoughtfully. His expertise in warfare was second to none. "Because of those archers on the hill, all my men could do was to wait in ambush. What's more, the way they had the mountain to their backs made our superior numbers count for nothing."

The group pondered over this for a moment.

"It's Abbas, isn't it?' Ibn Qamia blurted out. Abbas was not present at the meeting, even though he had a permanent seat at the table. Since becoming a secret Muslim, he'd been using the excuse of poor health to miss them. Each time he told the servant boy "Tell them I'm sick", he'd quietly tell himself, *but I am sick, sick of their idol worship.*

Ikrimah shook his head protesting, "A son of Abdul Muttalib? No, never. He's an honourable man."

"His brother, Abu Talib, helped Muhammad, didn't he? What makes you so sure Abbas isn't the same?" Ibn Qamia said before turning sharply to Abu Sufyan. "I bet he's hiding something," he said through gritted teeth. "I've never trusted him."

"You don't trust your own son," Amr ibn Aas grinned wryly, earning a roomful of chuckles and smirks.

Abu Sufyan rose to his feet once again. "I'm afraid I must leave," he said. He looked and sounded exhausted. "I have some important business to attend to."

"More important than *this*?!"

Too embarrassed to explain the real reason for his departure, he ignored the question. "Anyway, if what I say is true about there being a spy amongst us, considerable danger lies ahead." The men shifted awkwardly in their seats, and some even stood up. "And whether Uhud was truly a victory or not, one thing remains clear: This is not the end. We are still at war with the Muslims."

Cast of Characters

Character	Description	Full Arabic spelling
Abbas	The youngest of the Prophet's paternal uncles. He became Muslim and kept his Islam a secret.	*'Abbās*
Abul Aas	The Prophet's son in law, married to his eldest daughter Zaynab	*Abū al-'Āṣ ibn al-Rabī'*
Abdullah Ibn Ubay	Referred to as simply Ibn Ubay, he is the chief of the hypocrites in Madinah.	*'Abdullah ibn Ubayy*
Abu Amir	A nobleman of the Khazraj tribe who had left Madinah after the Muslim's victory at Badr. Nicknamed 'The Evil One' instead of 'the Noble One'	*Abu 'Āmir*
Abu Bakr	The Prophet's best friend and the first adult male to accept Islam.	*Abu Bakr as-Siddīq*
Abu Dujana	A Khazraj swordsman honoured with wielding a sword given by the Prophet Muhammad during the battle of Uhud. Known for his red bandana.	*Abu Dujānah*

Abu Jahl	Leader of the Makhzum Tribe of the Quraysh. The Prophet called him 'the Pharoah of this nation'.	*'Amr ibn Hishām al-Makhzūmī*
Abu Lahab	The Prophet's uncle and enemy of Islam.	*'Abd al-'Uzzā ibn 'Abd al-Muṭṭalib*
Abu Sufyan	A leader and merchant from the Quraysh. He was the general for the Quraysh at the battle of Uhud.	*Abu Sufyān ibn Harb*
Abu Talib	The Prophet's uncle and supporter. He is the father of Ali, and former leader of the Hashim Tribe.	*Abū Ṭālib ibn 'Abd al-Muṭṭalib*
Aisha	The wife of the Prophet, and daughter of Abu Bakr	*'Ā'isha bint Abi Bakr*
Ali	The cousin of the Prophet, and the first child to accept Islam.	*'Alī ibn Abī Ṭālib*
Amr ibn Aas	The statesman sent by the Quraysh to get the Muslims removed from Abyssinia	*'Amr ibn al-'Āṣ*
Atikah	The Prophet's aunt, and sister of Abbas	*'Ātikah*
Bilal	The first Abyssinian to embrace Islam, and the first *mu'azzin* (prayer caller).	*Bilāl ibn Rabah'*
Fatimah	Youngest daughter of the Prophet, also called Zahra, "the Radiant One".	Fāṭimah al-Zahrā'

Hamza	The Prophet's uncle, also known as 'The Lion of Allah'.	*Ḥamza ibn ʿAbd al-Muṭṭalib*
Hasan	Prophet Muhammad's grandson, son of Ali and Fatimah.	*Al-Ḥasan ibn ʿAli*
Hind	The wife of Abu Sufyan	*Hind bint ʿUtba*
Ibn Haram	An elderly companion from the Ansar, stricken with poverty, known for his sincere advice to Ibn Ubay	
Ibn Jubair	An expert bowman known for his bravery, appointed as the leader of the archers during the battle of Uhud	*ʿAbdullah ibn Jubair*
Ibn Masud	A Companion from the Muhajirun who had the honour of being the first to recite the Qur'an in front of the Ka'bah.	*ʿAbdullah ibn Masʿūd*
Ibn Qamia	A warrior from the Quraysh who threw a rock at the Prophet during the battle of Uhud	*ʿAbdullah ibn Qamiʾah*
Ibn Umm Maktum	A blind Companion who was appointed as the city's caretaker in the Prophet's absence	*ʿAbdullah ibn Umm Maktūm*
Ikrimah	The son of Abu Jahl	*Ikrimah ibn Abi Jahl*

Ka'b	A famous poet of the Khazraj Tribe who had embraced Islam during the Second Pledge of Aqabah	*Ka'b ibn Mālik*
Khadijah	The first wife of the Prophet, and the first woman to embrace Islam.	*Khadījah bint Khuwaylid*
Khalid bin Walid	An elite warrior who led the cavalry of the Quraysh at Uhud.	*Khālid bin Walīd*
Mus'ab	The first ambassador of Islam to Madinah. Also known as 'the first of the Muhajirun'.	*Mus'ab ibn 'Umayr*
Nusaybah	One of the women who witnessed the Second Aqabah treaty, a woman of the Khazraj Tribe known for her exceptional fighting and presence during battle of Uhud.	*Nusaybah bint Ka'b*
Rafi'	A young boy known for his archery, allowed to join Uhud.	

Rufaydah	Daughter of a renowned physician, first female Muslim doctor, who trained nurses and was in charge of the first health centre attached to the Prophet's Mosque.	*Rufaida al-Aslamia*
Ruqayya	Daughter of the Prophet and wife of Uthman.	*Ruayyah bint Muhammad*
Sa'd	A noble chief from the Ansar, first honoured with role of overseeing Madinah in the Prophet's absence	*Sa'd ibn Mu'āth*
Safiyyah	The Prophet's aunt, sister of Hamza and mother of Zubair	*Ṣafiyya bint 'Abd al-Muṭṭalib*
Safwan	A wealthy man of the Quraysh, and like his father Umayyah, he too was a big opponent of the Prophet.	*Safwān ibn Umayyah*
Samurah	A young orphan boy with wrestling skills allowed to join the battle of Uhud.	

Suraaqa	A renowned bounty hunter who had pursued the Prophet during the Hijra but ended up embracing Islam after witnessing miracles.	*Surāqa ibn Mālik*
Talha	A Companion who the Prophet praised as being 'a martyr walking the face of the earth'.	*Ṭalḥa ibn ʿUbayd Allāh*
Ubay	A companion known for being the best Qur'an reciter in Madinah	*Ubay ibn Kaʿb*
Ubaydah	The Prophet's cousin who was martyred at Badr	*ʿUbayda ibn al-Ḥārith*
Umar	The famous Companion and friend of the Prophet. Known as al-Faruq, the one who sets right from wrong.	*ʿUmar ibn al-Khaṭṭāb*
Umayr	A companion who was once an enemy of Islam but made it his life's mission to call others to Islam.	
Umayya	A chief of Quraysh who was responsible for oppressing Bilal when he was his slave master.	*Umayya ibn ʿAbd Shams*
Umm Ayman	A female companion and long-time motherly figure in the prophet's life.	

Umm Ma'bad	A Bedouin woman who embraced Islam, known for one of the most comprehensive narrations describing the prophet.	
Usayd	A leading tribesman of the Aws Tribe who had embraced Islam after hearing Mus'ab recite.	*Usayd ibn Ḥudayr*
Utbah	A chief of the Quraysh, father of Hind. He was killed during the Battle of Badr.	*'Utbah ibn Rabī'ah*
Uthman	The Prophet's son-in-law and close Companion, known for being wealthy, handsome, and generous.	*'Uthmān ibn 'Affān*
Wahshi	Abyssinian slave tasked with killing Hamza, known for being exceptionally skilled with a spear.	
Zubair	The Prophet's cousin, son of Safiyyah.	*Zubair ibn al-'Awwām*

Endnotes

1. As-Sīrah an-Nabawiyya by Ibn Kathir Vol 2 p. 170
2. Sahih Muslim, Ḥadīth no. 2564
3. Tirmidhi, Hadith no. 2487
4. Sahih al-Bukhari, Hadith no. 6372
5. Muhammad Hamidullah, The First Written Constitution in the World, 3rd ed. (Lahore: Sh. Muhammad Ashraf Publishers, 1975)
6. Abu Dawud, Hadith no. 3004
7. al-Raheeq al-Makhtoom by al-Mubarakpuri p. 196
8. Sahih Muslim, Hadith no. 1917
9. Ibn Hisham vol 2 p. 207
10. Ibn Hisham vol 2 p. 203
11. al-Tabaqaat al-Kubra by Ibn Sa'd vol 2 p. 252
12. As-Sīrah an-Nabawiyya by Ibn Kathir vol 2 p. 254
13. Seerah by Ibn Hisham, vol 2 p. 229
14. Sahih Muslim, Hadith no. 1763
15. Tafsīr Ibn Kathīr, Verse 44 of Surah al-Anfal
16. Seerah by Ibn Hisham vol 2 p.626
17. Sahih al-Bukhari 4026
18. Tirmidhi, Ḥadīth No. 1641
19. al-Bukhari, Ḥadīth No. 3130
20. Seerah by Ibn Hisham vol 2 p.661
21. Sahih Muslim, Hadith no. 2059
22. Sahih al-Bukhari, Hadith no. 174
23. Tabaqaat Ibn Sa'd, vol 8, p. 253
24. Al-Nasa'i, Hadith no. 5310
25. Tirmidhi, Hadith no. 3872
26. Musnad Imam Ahmad, Hadith no. 643
27. Tabaqat Ibn Sa'd, Vol 2 p. 268

28. Raheeq al-Makhtoom, p. 251

29. Musnad Ahmed, Hadith no. 14787

30. Musnad Ahmed, Hadith no. 15766

31. Sahih Muslim, Hadith no. 2827

32. Sunan Ibn Majah, Hadith no. 190

33. Sahih al-Bukhari, Hadith no. 2818

34. Sahih al-Bukhari, Hadith no. 3014

35. Dalaa'il an-Nubuwwa by al-Bayhaqi, Vol 3 p. 233

36. Sahih al-Bukhari, Hadith no. 4043

37. Tabaqaat Ibn Sa'd, Vol 2 p. 250

38. Tabaqaat Ibn Sa'd, Vol 2 p. 270

39. Ibn Hishaam, Vol 3 p. 91

40. Sahih Muslim, Hadith no. 1789

41. Sahih al-Bukhari, Hadith no. 3039

42. Musnad Imam Ahmad, Hadith no. 1418

43. Sahih al-Bukhari, Hadith no. 3897